Disorder in the Court

WITH RODNEY R. JONES AND GERALD F. UELMEN,
*Disorderly Conduct*

AS WINSTON SCHOONOVER,
*Wilkes: His Life and Crimes, A Novel*

# Disorder in the Court

. . . . . . . . . . . . . . . . . . . . . . . . . . . . . . . . . . .

## Great Fractured Moments In Courtroom History

**CHARLES M. SEVILLA**

W · W · NORTON & COMPANY · NEW YORK · LONDON

Copyright © 1992 by Charles M. Sevilla
Illustrations copyright © 1992 by Lee Lorenz
Printed in the United States of America

First published as a Norton paperback 1993; reissued 1999

The text of this book is composed in 12/14 Avanta, with the display set in
Mistral and Spectra Heavy. Manufacturing by the Haddon Craftsmen, Inc.

Library of Congress Cataloging in Publication Data
Sevilla, Charles M.
Disorder in the court: great fractured moments in courtroom
history / by Charles M. Sevilla.
p.   cm.
Excerpts from the author's column, Great moments in courtroom
history.
1. Trials—United States—Anecdotes.   2. Courts—United States—
Anecdotes.   3. Law—United States—Anecdotes.   I. Title.
K184.S48   1992
347.73'1—dc20
[347.3071]        91–40416

ISBN 0-393-31928-8

W. W. Norton & Company, Inc.
500 Fifth Avenue, New York, N.Y. 10110
www.wwnorton.com

W. W. Norton & Company Ltd.
Castle House, 75/76 Wells Street, London W1T 3QT

6 7 8 9 0

# CONTENTS

# INTRODUCTION

Joseph Conrad described life as birth and death separated by struggle. For me, humor has been the lubricant to make the struggle a bit less rough, a survival instinct against life's rigors.

Striving to see humor in the world in childhood helped me cope with my many inadequacies: like catching a football with my mouth in the third grade (I not only failed, I lost part of a tooth), or getting picked off first base in Little League and not even knowing it, or having my fourth-grade girlfriend swear "eternal love" which lasted only until the afternoon recess.

You had to laugh so as not to cry. I did both. That was all long before law school. In fact, were it not for its pre-law honing, I think that whatever sense of humor I had would have been suffocated to extinction in the numbing, obscure, and far too serious world that was my law school education.

Law school was a procession of nauseatingly overwritten rubbish, like the following sample discussing the doctrine of double jeopardy:

There must be some legal necessity basic to one acquittal, not involved in the next trial, to justify a superseding convic-

tion. We cannot permit initial trial deficiencies to be cured
by subsequent trials. There are only four quarters to a football game. The exorcised double jeopardy is the constitu-
tional eliminator of the might have beens. Puristic parallel-
ism is not an absolute in the law of double jeopardy.
Multitudinous criminal charges may spring from the same
incident. The State's argument in the present case would
nullify the doctrine of double jeopardy because any slight
deviation in the indictment would give the State another
Monday morning quarter.
     *Johnson v. Estelle,* 506 F.2d 347 (5th Cir. 1975)


This was the standard fare. The study of dirt would
have been more interesting. This dulling experience
only enhanced my search for humor over the years of
my legal education and practice. I have collected tran-
scripts of cases that either ring a funny note or are
ridiculous or absurd. For many, you had to be there. (I
tried to eliminate the latter from this collection.)
     For the past twelve years I have written a column
with the pompous title of "Great Moments in Courtroom History" where many of the offerings reprinted
here first appeared. Those columns have been running
in the *Forum* and *Champion,* and I have many thanks
to give the members of the California Attorneys for
Criminal Justice and the National Association of Criminal Defense Lawyers for their continued contributions
to the column and to the organizations which have
kept the column in print.
     The magazine column has thrived because the read-
ers have sent me their own favorites, which then became the grist for future columns. My only editing has

been to remove the names of the guilty parties, to add identifying words to aid comprehension, and to trim the prose (you may be surprised to learn that lawyers can be verbose, a malady that has as its source getting paid by the hour).

Also, as you will read from these excerpts, the work of the criminal lawyer often involves a courtroom argot that might be thought more appropriate to a shipyard locker room. Where the wording is raunchy, I have keyed the selection with an asterisk so that the squeamish may look away, and everyone else can head straight for those passages.

A previous batch of these "Great Moments in Courtroom History" may be found in *Disorderly Conduct* (1987), a W. W. Norton publication which combined my collection with those of my co-editors, Dean Gerald Uelman of the University of Santa Clara Law School and attorney Rod Jones.

My thanks go to my wife Donna for her help in assembling the manuscript. Also, many thanks to my editor Hilary Hinzmann of Norton and my literary agent Joe Vallely, for their advice and support. My apologies to those early contributors whose identities I lost and who are now given my equivalent *nom de plume* of Anonymous Bosch, of Paris, Idaho (and a few other pseudonyms).

Enjoy.

# Disorder in the Court

# 1

## DEFENDANTS SAY
## THE DAMNDEST THINGS

*"His first two clients were the last two persons hanged in the Maycomb County jail. Atticus had urged them to accept the state's generosity in allowing them to plead guilty to second-degree murder and escape with their lives, but they were Haverfords, in Maycomb County a name synonymous with jackass. The Haverfords had dispatched Maycomb's leading blacksmith in a misunderstanding arising from the alleged wrongful detention of a mare, were imprudent enough to do it in the presence of three witnesses, and insisted that the-son-of-a-bitch-had-it-coming-to-him was good enough defense for anybody."*
### HARPER LEE, TO KILL A MOCKINGBIRD

*"Defense Counsel compliments the Public Prosecutor on his brilliant presentation of the indictment; the Public Prosecutor expresses his admiration for the Defense Counsel's eloquence; the Presiding Judge congratulates both speakers; in short, everyone is more than satisfied . . . except the accused."*
### HONORÉ DAUMIER, LAWYERS AND JUSTICE, NO. 16

"*You have heard testimony that the day in question was cold, windy, and with above-average precipitation. Do you still maintain it was a nice day?*"

# PRO PER MOTION
*(E. Grossman, Berkeley)*

THE COURT    Do you understand, sir, that if I permit
you to represent yourself, it will be
without the assistance of an attorney and
that you're going to be held to all the
technical rules of evidence in criminal
procedure?

DEFENDANT    Yeah. I'll have to stop at the library and
get a book on law.

THE COURT    And you understand you will get access
to the jail library?

DEFENDANT    Yeah.

THE COURT    Do you understand that the case as
presented by the State will be handled
by an experienced district attorney who's
very specialized in the area of criminal
law, who has had extensive court trials
and jury trials, and that you won't be
entitled to any special consideration?

DEFENDANT    All I really need is the Constitution, the

Bill of Rights, a Holy Bible and a handgun.

## DEJA VU ALL OVER AGAIN
### *(Charles Coe, Anchorage, AK)*

DEFENDANT    I remember when I was in your courtroom in 1956 when you was a municipal judge.

THE COURT    I don't think we should go into that.

DEFENDANT    Not guilty, too.

THE COURT    Well, we all make mistakes, sir, but you didn't make one.

DEFENDANT    Well, you made one. I was guilty.

## FREE DUMB
### *(Kenneth Lezin, San Fernando)*

DA    Okay. How much earlier had you used cocaine?

DEFENDANT    I was getting high all that day.

DA    All right. So you were using cocaine. Were you free-basing cocaine?

DEFENDANT    No. I bought it.

THE COURT    We can put that one in the judicial humor book.

## THE GREAT TRAIN TRACK ROBBERY
### *(Keith Monroe, Santa Ana)*

**DA**   In August, you were again convicted of a federal offense, correct? And you were trying to steal a railroad?

**DEFENDANT**   That's what they said.

**DA**   Were you trying to steal a railroad?

**DEFENDANT**   About the only thing I would be stealing would be the tracks of the train. I didn't have a truck big enough to haul the railroad off.

**DA**   So what did you end up stealing?

**DEFENDANT**   The tracks.

## USES OF LANGUAGE⋆
### *(Keith Arthur, Stockton, CA)*

**THE COURT**   You were picked up on a new 245?

**DEFENDANT**   I don't know if it was 245, 645, 345. They picked me up on something, all right? Okay? Then when they also had me on that, he gave me a motherfucking charge for prostitution.

**COUNSEL**   Don't use language like that to the judge.

**DEFENDANT**   Prostitution? What? Prostitution? What you want me to say? They picked me up for prostitution.

## LOOSE LIPS*
### (Robert Calhoun, Jr., San Francisco)

Q. What was her response to that information?

A. She said she would take the child if she couldn't have her visit with him.

Q. Were those her exact words?

A. Her exact words were she would take the fucking kid.

DEFENDANT I never said that. You're a fucking liar!


## HONEST THIEF WITH SPECIALTY
### (Jeffrey Kay, Fort Lauderdale)

Q. Are you presently employed?

A. No.

Q. When was the last time you were employed?

A. I was self-employed.

Q. When?

A. When? All my life.

Q. What was the nature of your self-employment?

A. I was a thief.

Q. And did you have a particular specialty as a thief?

A. Burglar.

## INGRATIATING TESTIMONY
### *(Alan Ross, Miami)*

Q. You think that is funny?

A. Yes, sir. Because you are trying to put that thing on me and it ain't going to work.

Q. Let me ask you this: In addition to the things you have already told us about yourself, that is, you are an admitted perjurer, an admitted liar, you are also a three-time convicted felon?

A. Yes.

Q. You hit a state trooper over the head with a gun and left him in the trunk to die, all these things about yourself, is there anything else you want these twelve people to know about you to ingratiate yourself to them so they will believe you?

A. No.


## OUT OF IT
### *(Mark Arnold, Woodland, CA)*

Q. Do you recall telling the police that you passed out at that time?

A. I passed out, yes. I passed out. I think I blacked out. I passed out, but I don't know if I was really out. I just remember blacking out, and I assume I passed out,

or if I didn't pass out, I just blacked out
in my mind.


## SAY WHAT?
*(Gary Scherotter, Palm Springs)*

Q. I said: Did you tell the officer that you
   had only known him for one month?
A. At that time, yes.
Q. But that was not true, is it?
A. I said—okay. I said that because, you
   know, why should I like, tell you—no,
   okay. Okay. I sit back because, you know,
   when he asked me, "How long have you
   known him?" I was really just—because
   when I met him, I really didn't know
   him. So I had known him really well for
   a month or so. But I knew him, you
   know, for like two or three months—to
   be like friends.


## SAINT MARY
*(Juan Gonzales, Beeville, TX)*

Q. Now concerning this Don Pedrito
   Jaramillo Shrine in Falfurrias, Texas, what
   is the significance of this shrine in that
   community?

A.    In our case, we would ask it to help us cross over the border with this marijuana on this deal. I would light a candle. That's the best I can do, sir.

# TO ERR IS HUMAN, BUT ONLY MISDEMEANORS
### *(Hon. Marvin Aspen, Chicago)*

**DEFENDANT**    Your Honor. I just want to say that what I did I know was wrong, but I didn't know the extent of the sentence and stuff.

**THE COURT**    You didn't know what?

**DEFENDANT**    I didn't know that I could get involved like this. I thought it was just a misdemeanor or something like that, and if I got caught they would just suspend my food stamps for a while and I would go back. I didn't understand the law. That's the reason why I have always lived according to the law, but I made a mistake and I'm sorry.

**THE COURT**    In other words, you would commit the crime if it was a misdemeanor but not if it's a felony, is that right?

**DEFENDANT**    Not if it's a felony.

## WHAT IT IS
### (Ronald Smith, Beverly Hills)

Q. First of all, I need to ask you if you understand what a jury trial is, just as you've had in this case. Do you understand what a jury trial is?

DEFENDANT  Yeah, a jury trial is twelve ignorant people that is illiterate of the law.


## AGAINST ALL ODDS
### (Marty Costello, Merced, CA)

THE COURT  Now, you are entitled to a speedy and public trial by jury or by court. You know what a jury trial is?

DEFENDANT  Yes.

THE COURT  What's a jury trial?

DEFENDANT  A jury trial, twelve people find you guilty.

THE COURT  Yeah, that is about right. On occasion they find you not guilty, but—

DEFENDANT  I don't want to find out.

THE COURT  All right. A court trial is a judge sitting alone hearing your case.

DEFENDANT  I know that, too.

THE COURT  And he usually finds you guilty, too.

DEFENDANT  Yeah. So it is thirteen against one in other words.

THE COURT  Well—

DEFENDANT     With the district attorney it is about fifteen to one.

## POLICE REPORT
### (Tim Murphy, Los Angeles)

I observed defendant driving without headlights on. Defendant's vehicle was swaying from westbound curb lane to eastbound #1. As defendant's vehicle passed, I observed defendant with a large dog helping defendant drive (dog had front paws on steering wheel, possibly trying to save its own life). Upon stopping defendant's vehicle, defendant began yelling, "F--- Skippy [the dog]. You really got me f---ed this time." Skippy had no statement.

## I'M INNOCENT,
## I HIT THE SKINNY DUDE
### (Bob Boyce, San Diego)

*Defendant's statement to police*

It was my homies. Then other people came and started talking crazy and I got mad. I might have hit somebody, but it was a nice little skinny dude. I hear the guy who got beat up was a fat dude. I did not hit any big fat dudes, only the skinny dude. I was at the beach eating barbecued ribs when this whole thing happened.

## AUDIBLE ANSWER
*(Paul R. Huscher, Des Moines)*

THE COURT   Okay. Now, let me ask you again, had you been drinking that day? Alcohol, I mean?
DEFENDANT   Uh-huh.
THE COURT   Had you?
COUNSEL   Answer it audibly.
THE COURT   Had you been drinking alcohol that day?
DEFENDANT   Audibly.
THE COURT   What were you drinking, beer or what?
DEFENDANT   Uh-huh.
THE COURT   Beer?
COUNSEL   Answer him audibly.
DEFENDANT   Audibly.

## YELLOW JACKET
*(Julie Macek, Great Falls, MT)*

THE COURT   Do you have a coat, Mr. J.?
MR. J.   Your Honor, I was stung twice in the mouth by a yellow jacket a bit ago, and lost my coat. I don't know where it is, I am kind of getting my wits back.
THE COURT   You were being pursued by a yellow jacket and lost your coat in the process?
MR. J.   I am kind of coming out of it. I had something to eat, and took an antihistamine.

THE COURT  Are you allergic to a yellow jacket sting?

MR. J.  No more than normal. I had a paralysis in my mouth. I was kind of confused, and I really don't know where I left my jacket.

THE COURT  Are you prepared to go forward with these motions?

MR. J.  Yes.

THE COURT  Let's take up the motion to continue first.

MR. J.  I still don't feel entirely comfortable, Judge. I swallowed the yellow jacket and he got me twice on the tongue. He paid with his life.


## PRO PER STRIKES AGAIN
### *(Frederick Finn, Detroit)*

*Questions by the defendant*

Q.  Isn't it true, Kelly, that—Oh, let me ask it this way. Can you tell the Court the reasons why your family didn't like me?

A.  Just the way you were.

Q.  Tell us. Be explicit. How was I?

A.  You're just—

Q.  Just what?

A.  An asshole. How else can I put it?

Q.  That's an opinion. I want an answer.

THE COURT  That's the answer. You asked her what her opinion was and she told you.

DEFENDANT   Okay, okay. We'll go with that.
Q.   (by the Defendant) Why am I an asshole?


# DEVIL INSIDE
*(Lance Rogers, Washington, DC)*

Q.   Well, were you referring to cigarettes at that time?
A.   I was referring to I am not an angel.
Q.   Were you referring to stealing cigarettes at that time?
A.   I was referring to I am not an angel.
Q.   I will ask one more time. Were you referring to stealing cigarettes, yes or no?
A.   I am telling you what I was referring to.
THE COURT   Answer that question.
A.   Yes.
Q.   And that's all you were referring to is cigarettes?
A.   Not all.
Q.   What else were you referring to?
A.   I was referring to that I was not an angel.

# TWO POUNDS
*(Mari Morsell, West Los Angeles)*

THE COURT   The question is, do you think you are
            capable of thinking clearly today? I mean,
            you are indicating you are, but I have
            seen you stagger around the courtroom.

DEFENDANT   Hot damn. I thought I had been sitting
            all this time.

THE COURT   Talk to your lawyer.

DEFENDANT   The cops at jail say they know more
            than you do. I was in the hole for five
            days, allowed no phone calls, not allowed
            my constitutional rights. I was freezing
            cold. They wouldn't give me clothes.
            Then, I was put into a heat room. I was
            covered up in a cell. I called you. I
            called President Reagan. I called Justice
            O'Connor. I called John Glenn. I didn't
            get sleep or food, no medical attention,
            no psychiatric care, no medical care.
            Animals live better than this. I went
            back to jail, back to the hole, deprived of
            food, deprived of warmth, deprived of
            courtesy, deprived of respect, hauled
            around in buses, manhandled by officers,
            almost thrown through a windshield,
            deprived of phone calls, no lawyers,
            twenty-six days, no response from the
            Justice Department, no response from
            John Glenn, who went to the moon,

back to Metro, back to jail, back to, back
to, back to.

How much do you want out of this pound
of flesh, baby?


## THE PLEA
*(Lance Rogers, Washington, DC)*


THE COURT   Mr. E., you're charged here with driving
a motor vehicle under the influence of
alcohol. How do you plead, guilty or not
guilty?

MR. E.   I'm guilty as hell.

THE COURT   Let the record reflect the defendant is
guilty as hell.


## COOL UNDER FIRE
*(Anonymous Bosch, Paris, ID)*


A second telephone conversation took place between
defendant and one Howard Spector, a neighbor. At
the request of one of the officers Spector telephoned
defendant and said: "Jack you are making quite a dis-

turbance; I'm having a hard time studying." Defendant replied: "Howard, I'd like to talk to you but I'm real busy right now."* [From the opinion in *People v. Hoxie* 252 C.A.2d 901, 904 (1967)]

## THE BEGINNER
*(Otha Standifer, III, Los Angeles)*

COUNSEL  Have you ever been convicted of a felony?
A. Yes.
Q. How many?
A. One, so far.

## SUPER-NOVA
*(Anonymous Bosch, Paris, ID)*

COUNSEL  Just a minute, Your Honor. Your Honor, I'd like to state for the record the defendant is now requesting me to request the Court to allow him to ask a question.
THE COURT  Why do you feel I should do that?
DEFENDANT  Since my attorney won't ask the

*The house was [then] being besieged by forty to fifty officers. Between 300 and 500 rounds of ammunition were expended. Eventually twenty-six rounds of tear-gas ammunition were fired.

question—says it might not be any good—I will take the consequences of it. He feels in his judgment it is probably not good for me.

THE COURT  Do you understand that you are going directly opposed to what your attorney is advising you?

DEFENDANT  Sure.

THE COURT  You are the one who is going to suffer.

DEFENDANT  I am the one going to Superior Court.

THE COURT  I don't know whether it will go, but you are not going to be able to come back later and say that you—

DEFENDANT  I hardly ever do that in court, Your Honor. I put it on appeal, Your Honor.

THE COURT  I understand. I am well aware of that.

DEFENDANT  I figured you were.

THE COURT  Do you understand you can't claim inadequacy of counsel or that you didn't have proper advice if I allow you to go ahead and ask some questions; you are stuck with whatever comes out?

DEFENDANT  Sure.

THE COURT  All right. Go ahead.

DEFENDANT  (to the witness) What time was it when you went out the store door when I supposedly ran out with some shirts?

A.  A little after eight.

Q.  What kind of car was it—make, not model?

A.  It was a Ford.

Q.  You just stated it was a Nova.

A.  When it was leaving.

Q.  When it was leaving, it was a Nova, and when it was parked it was a Ford?

A.  To my knowledge when it was parked.

Q.  You didn't get the color?

A.  No.

Q.  You got bad eyes?

DA  Objection. Argumentative.

THE COURT  Sustained. I thought you wanted to ask one question. What is it you are trying to do now?

DEFENDANT  Your Honor, to establish a foundation if he saw what he saw. He saw a Ford. He saw a Nova. I only own a Nova.


# DA AS STUDENT;
# DEFENDANT AS TEACHER
*(Susan Rutberg, San Francisco)*


Q.  Drugs cost a lot of money, don't they?

A.  Not really. Some of them do, some of them don't.

Q.  Cocaine is pretty expensive?

A.  Cocaine is rather expensive.

Q.  $100, $125 a gram?

A.  Lady, you're buying it from the wrong person if you're paying that much.

Q.  How about a discount? Around $80?

A.  That's a little better.

## SEARCH AND SEIZURE*
### (Sam Polverino, Santa Clara)

Q. At that point it is your testimony that she [the officer] reached in with her left hand, inside of your pants?

A. She was fondling me, you know. We were playing, you know. We were goofing around. She was fondling me and it took her a little while, but she found it.

THE COURT Would you clarify that, please?

Q. Found what?

A. Found the wallet.


## HAZEL AND BILL
### (John Hud, Los Angeles)

THE COURT Hazel?

BILL Do you want my wife up here?

THE COURT You are not Hazel; are you?

BILL Hardly. That's my wife.

THE COURT Hazel, and William.

BILL That's me.

THE COURT William, did you get your driver's license yet?

BILL No, sir.

THE COURT They are not going to give it to you, are they?

BILL No, they are not. I am not driving. The car is downstairs being checked. She is doing the driving.

| | |
|---|---|
| THE COURT | She is driving? |
| BILL | Yes, I am not driving. |
| THE COURT | Has that car been corrected? |
| BILL | Yes, sir. Would you like to come down and examine it? It is in the back. Remember the agreement we made? |
| THE COURT | Yes. |
| BILL | If it all works fine, we are happy. If it doesn't, you put her [Hazel] in jail and I go to the first bar and have a beer. Don't put that down. |
| THE COURT | Don't put that down. |
| BILL | I am a little shy. So don't be worried. I am not driving. She is driving. The car is downstairs. It is all ready for your personal inspection or otherwise. We finally found where to park after all this trip. |
| THE COURT | Where did you park? |
| BILL | We have been parking in this public parking up on the highway right on Main Street. Hazel walked down here. It is a long way. And I have been waiting in the beer joint. |
| THE COURT | How many beers have you had? |
| BILL | None yet. I had a Bloody Mary and she had coffee. Every morning I have one or two Bloody Marys. (Whereupon Hazel touches Bill's arm and shakes head negatively.) |
| BILL (TO HAZEL) | I am telling the truth. What do you want me to do? Tell him I am a |

THE COURT / BILL dialogue:

teetotaler? Anybody who drinks coffee can suck eggs. I have never tried that. Do you want to examine our car? She is the driver, if you want to see the driver's license. You come down and I will meet you at the beer joint.

THE COURT What time?

BILL I knew you were the right judge. We have been in every courtroom in here. In fact, I almost went in the ladies' restroom. Boy, I try. We are downstairs if you would like to come.

THE COURT We'll see you, Hazel and Bill.

BILL Well, God bless you. You sure kept your word. See how you talk to a gentleman, Hazel? He is not scared of me and I am sure as hell scared of him. Let's get out of here before he changes his mind.

THE COURT See you soon.

BILL I hope not. I don't want to see you for a while; not until my wife stops drinking. You owe me twenty bucks, Hazel.

# 2

# THE LAWYERS

*"An advocate who has been well paid in advance will find the cause he is pleading all the more just."*

PASCAL

*"Woe unto you also, ye lawyers! For ye lade men with burdens grievous to be borne, and ye yourselves touch not the burdens with one of your fingers."*

LUKE 11:46

*"For the last time, learned counsel will stop sparring with the prosecuting attorney."*

# THE ORDER

A prominent Manhattan lawyer was arraigned in Manhattan Criminal Court yesterday on charges of impersonating Lenox Hill Hospital doctors and ordering unneeded enemas for patients. . . . Hospital personnel followed [his] orders.

*N.Y. Newsday,* 10/16/90

# THE MESSAGE
*(Howard Price, Beverly Hills)*

COUNSEL     I would like to say that the reason that I did not show up to court is that before I am a lawyer I am a servant of the Lord Jesus Christ and everything I do is subject to Him, and He told me. . . .

THE COURT     Who told you?

COUNSEL     Jesus Christ.

THE COURT     He told you?

COUNSEL   That I should not go to court on
          Thursday or Friday and that He
          instructed me not to even call in on
          Friday, and that is why I did not come
          in, and when He allows me to come in,
          I come in. I go where He allows me to
          go and I do what He tells me to do. I
          cannot let any court supersede that. That
          is a right set up by the founding fathers
          of this country.

THE COURT What is the message today?

COUNSEL   The message today was to come in.

THE COURT As of now, the message is going to be
          that you are going into custody.


## CLOSING ARGUMENT
*(Don Holt, Florence, AL)*

DA        Ladies and gentlemen, the defendant in
          this case can be analogized to a duck
          because there's an old saying that if it
          walks like a duck, quacks like a duck,
          and looks like a duck, it must be a duck,
          and the same argument can be made as
          it would relate to drunks and that's what
          the defendant in this case is.

COUNSEL   Ladies and gentlemen, I deeply resent
          the characterization that the prosecutor
          has made of my client. My client is
          neither a duck nor a drunk. What the

prosecutor has done in this case is create a hybrid bird that is a cross between a pheasant and a duck. I cannot pronounce the name of the new species but it is spelled P-H-U-C-K, and that is exactly what the prosecution is trying to give my client in this case.

### ONE-SIDED
*(Thomas A. Corfman, Chicago)*

DA   Judge, I would object to Counsel's characterization of this disagreement. He is giving a one-sided view.

THE COURT   Of course he is. That is what you expect of a trial attorney.

### THE TRUTH STOPS HERE
*(Michael Davis, Dardanelle, AR)*

COUNSEL   Well, our objection, Your Honor, and I want to make this very clear, is that there's a time that truth has to stop, and that time—

THE COURT   Why does it have to stop?

COUNSEL   Because the trial has started.

## CROSS-EXAMINATION
*(Tom Lundy, Sacramento)*

THE COURT   Please begin.

COUNSEL   Thank you.

Q.   (to witness) Miss, while you have, if you do have—you still—oh, you don't.

THE COURT   That was a great start, Counsel.

## TOUCHÉ
*(Michael J. Kennedy, Joshua Tree, CA)*

A.   You mumbled on the first part of that and I couldn't understand what you were saying. Could you repeat the question?

Q.   I mumbled, did I? Well, we'll just ask the court reporter to read back what I said. She didn't indicate any problem understanding what I said, so obviously she understood every word. We'll just have her read my question back and find out if there was any mumbling going on. Madam reporter, would you be so kind?

COURT REPORTER   Mumble, mumble, mumble, mumble, mumble.

## DIRTY OLD MAN
*(Gary Nichols, Ventura, CA)*

COUNSEL    In the *Martinez* case, the Court of Appeal does an excellent historical review of kidnapping statutes starting at the time dirt was invented. It talks about the kidnapping statutes prior to 1933. . . .

THE COURT    I was born in 1934.

COUNSEL    Well, dirt was invented before then, Your Honor.

## ANSWER TO THE QUESTION
*(Scott Tilson, Minneapolis)*

THE COURT    Are all three of the defendants black?

COUNSEL #1    My client is white.

COUNSEL #2    My client is described in the police report as mulatto.

THE COURT    How do you describe her?

COUNSEL #2    Pregnant.

## FORGET SOMETHING?*
*(Marcus Peppard, Richmond, VA)*

COUNSEL    Your Honor, the defense would argue the People haven't proved the prior conviction.

DA  Oh shit!
COUNSEL  That's a legal term?
THE COURT  One used quite often in law school.

## MEANING OF
## THE CONSTITUTION
*(Steven Wax, Portland, OR)*

Q.  In the course of your years practicing as an attorney, did you have problems with alcohol from time to time?

A.  Yes.

DA  Objection. Move to strike.

THE COURT  On what grounds?

DA  It's irrelevant. And I might define for the Court, since I think there are going to be a substantial number of these objections, that it's the State's position that an attorney who has an IQ of 41, who has barely passed the Bar, and who has fouled up every other case they have ever tried is still perfectly capable of giving adequate legal services within the meaning of the Constitution.

## RX FOR THE DA
*(Kevin McCoy, Kenai, AK)*

DA    Now that he has been convicted, there is even stronger need for him to go ahead and get this sentence done. My concern is, number one, that there are no grounds for the appeal and it's just going to be used—as Counsel said as he headed out the door after the jury verdict—it's going to be used to delay the proceedings.

COUNSEL    I never said that to her. . . . I take strong opposition to the statement as to what I allegedly said because I never said that. I don't know what the DA's been smoking but she ain't remembering very good.

DA    Your Honor, I can quote Counsel after we went off the record at the jury trial. He said, "We can jam this on appeal for at least a year." Number one, it's unethical to try to delay things, and number two, there's no grounds for the appeal. He's just trying to postpone the inevitable that his client is going to be facing in getting treatment.

COUNSEL    I still take strong objection and disagree as to what she said and think she has got a hold of some good dope out of the evidence locker.

DA    Your Honor, I object to his claiming that

I have been committing crimes. I think
it is strongly objectionable and unethical
and I object to that.

COUNSEL    I take it back, maybe it was prescription
drugs.

## A HOUSE IS NOT A HOME
*(Kelvin Filer, Compton, CA)*

DA    Your Honor, if he testified that he lived
at the bus station, he wouldn't necessarily
have an expectation of privacy.

THE COURT    If he testified he lived at the bus
station—you're right. You may be right.

DA    What I'm trying to find out is whether
or not this house was a bus station.

## INFLAMMATORY
*(Roger Vehr, Fresno)*

Q.    Did you observe anything?
A.    Yes, we did.
Q.    When we found the vehicle, we saw
several unusual items in the car in the
right front floorboard of the vehicle.
There was what appeared to be a
Molotov cocktail, a green bottle—

COUNSEL    Objection. I'm going to object to that
word, Molotov cocktail.

THE COURT    What is your legal objection, Counsel?
COUNSEL    It's inflammatory, Your Honor.


## NO FLACCID PENIS
## DEFENSE HERE*
*(Marcia Levine, Los Angeles)*

Your Honor, you have tried rape cases either in private practice or on the bench, and you know what a gang rape looks like. It's not superficial injuries to a face. It's fractured mandibles, ripped-up clothes, it's ripped-up uteruses. That's what a gang rape is. Now, how do you get around it? They have created from imagination what we call the flaccid penis defense. When you get on the stand, make sure you say none of these guys could get it up. That's the only way out. Well, I can have both boys, Your Honor, if you clear the courtroom, spring a hard-on eight inches long, and you know it.


## ONE LOUSY HAIRCUT
*(Frank O'Connor, Shasta)*

DA    Your Honor, for the record, I would like to note that the last time I was in court with the defendant, the defendant did not have a haircut. He has had a haircut in the meantime. Just like that on the record.

| | |
|---|---|
| Counsel #1 | There's nothing illegal about that, is there? |
| The Court | It's on the record. That's all I know about it. |
| Counsel #1 | I had a haircut last week. |
| Counsel #2 | I'm planning on getting a haircut next week. |
| Counsel #3 | I got one yesterday. |
| Counsel #1 | May I make an inquiry as to the court reporter? |
| The Court | I was just going to ask. |

## DRAWING A PICTURE*
*(Gene Miller, Riverside, CA)*

| | |
|---|---|
| Counsel | But you were able to see his penis? |
| Witness | I saw the shape of it like a shadow. That's how I saw him, too. |
| Counsel | Well, I want to try to determine whether he was—whether the assailant's penis was circumcised or not. Let me ask you this. Do you know what a German helmet looks like? |
| Witness | (No response). |
| Counsel | Do you know what a foreskin is? |
| Witness | (Witness shakes head back and forth). |
| Counsel | I will draw a diagram and ask you to compare what it looks like. Okay? |
| Witness | (Nods up and down). |
| Counsel | (Draws pictures). |

THE COURT  It's obvious that art was not one of your major subjects, Counsel.

COUNSEL (TO WITNESS)  Did it look like it was wearing a German helmet or a turtleneck sweater?

## CLOSING ARGUMENTS
*(Christopher Armen, Los Angeles)*

COUNSEL  I ask you once again, as I close, merely to do what is correct in this case, which is to find my client innocent because he is in fact innocent. At the same time, you must punish the police because you are the watchers of the watchman and the way to punish the police is to throw out both of these charges. Thank you.

THE COURT  All right. Mr. Prosecutor, you may close.

DA  I suppose you ought to give him the dope and the machine gun back and an apology, and send him out the door. I suppose that's what we ought to do. We just hand it back to him and say, "I'm sorry, sir, take it all back. The cops fabricated this entire thing." This is so ludicrous, I want to puke.

## SO STIPULATED
*(Barry Collins, Santa Monica)*

DA    Did the defendant make any other statements to you at that time?

WITNESS    He told me he had the best lawyer in Los Angeles and that I didn't have a case.

COUNSEL    I'll stipulate to that, Your Honor.


## VIGOROUS ADVOCACY
*(Anonymous Bosch, Paris, ID)*

In closing argument, the prosecutor referred to the three defense attorneys as the "unholy alliance" who had themselves inflicted wounds on their client to create evidence to support a self-defense theory.

*State v. Alsup,* 69 Nev. 121 (1952)


## THE BOW TIE CHALLENGE★

At the conclusion of the hearing, FBI Agent L. approached Defense Counsel and stated, "I ought to take off your tie and shove it up your ass." Defense Counsel responded by inviting L. to step outside the courtroom.

The incident was reported to the Court by Counsel, who suggested Agent L.'s behavior was intended to intimidate the defendant or his counsel and to interfere with the defendant's right to representation. The Court directed the parties to submit suggestions on the action, if any, to be taken by the Court.

Agent L. is an experienced FBI agent. Defense Counsel, an able attorney with a jovial personality whose in-court manner can be characterized as that of an exuberant gladiator, has a penchant for bow ties. He played football at the University of Kansas and is approximately ten years younger and 40 pounds heavier than Agent L.

Agent L.'s unprovoked conduct in the courtroom raises questions not only as to his training and ability as an FBI agent but also as to his judgment and belief in his own physical capabilities. In light of Defense Counsel's strongly stated disclaimer that any intended intimidation was effective, the Court finds that the quality of the defense afforded the defendant has not been jeopardized.

The Court finds further that perhaps the appropriate sanction would be simply to direct Agent L. to attempt to carry out his threat. While Defense Counsel might be willing to "participate" in the imposition of this sanction as evidenced by his response to Agent L., the Court concludes that such sanction might very well constitute cruel and unusual punishment in contravention of the Eighth Amendment to the United States Constitution.

An order issued by the U.S. District Court for Western District of Oklahoma

## HOT UNDER THE COLLAR
*(James E. McCready, San Francisco)*

THE COURT    One other thing. Is there some reason
             why your tie is not against your neck and
             hangs down loose and your collar is
             unbuttoned?

COUNSEL      There is a reason.

THE COURT    State the reason.

COUNSEL      The reason my collar is undone is there
             is no button. Secondly, I think the tie is
             where it should be. I don't know how to
             make it bigger or tighter.

THE COURT    It wasn't earlier. It may be tighter. I'm
             going to order that you go out and buy a
             shirt tonight even if you have to buy one
             with a button on it that will fit around
             your neck so tomorrow you can have
             your shirt properly attached at the top to
             provide an appearance of professionalism
             in the courtroom.

COUNSEL      My hair is unkempt and my suits don't
             fit right. I don't think that I would
             project professionalism. I don't think that
             I will; that is not me. I don't think the
             tie is going to do that. If the Court
             wants me to do it, I should get a
             haircut.

THE COURT    The Court will not make you get a
             haircut. Wear your hair any way you like.
             You will not wear a tie around your neck
             loosened with the collar wide open. We

don't allow jurors to come in T-shirts or shorts to feel comfortable.

COUNSEL    I will have a shirt tomorrow.


## MOVE TO STRIKE
### *(Milton Hirsch, Miami)*

COUNSEL    (to DA) Don't do that again. You are making faces. Don't move your head in a nonverbal assertive conduct manner.

DA    Let the record reflect that the prosecutor has now belted the defense attorney across the chest.
(Thereupon, the prosecutor belted Defense Counsel across the chest.)


## BUTTING HEADS
### *(Robert Kimmel, Pensacola)*

COUNSEL A.    I object to Mr. B., number one, calling me an asshole before this deposition.

COUNSEL B.    My silence will never be interpreted as acquiescence, and there are at least five or six other people that had to be present during this alleged statement, and have you seen the shrink lately? I called you a what before the deposition today? Was that in this room? Maybe two years

ago, I might have. Do you mean—when
you made that allegation, you are saying
I said what in this room?

COUNSEL A.  My deposition is not being taken.

COUNSEL B.  You had better tell me what you are
accusing me of calling you right now.

COUNSEL A.  My deposition is not being taken.

COUNSEL B.  There are a whole bunch of enemies in
this room as far as litigation is
concerned. I would like to ask all my
enemies that I sue daily and try to smash
into bits and expect them to smash me
into bits, legally and ethically, did anyone
hear what this man alleges I said? I
swear to God, I didn't say it. Did you
hear me say it, sir? Did you hear me say
it?

COURT REPORTER  I am not an attorney. I cannot be on
the record.

COUNSEL B.  You are a human being who has ears.
Did you hear me say it? I have never
said that, and when we finish this, we
are going to ask for an apology, sir,
because that is a lie and if you want to
do something about my calling you a liar,
I will be right outside when this
deposition is finished.

COUNSEL A.  I would ask that the deposition please
proceed.

COUNSEL B.  If you do it again, I will do something
about it.

COUNSEL C.   By the time we get outside, everybody will be too tired to fight.


# WHY I WAS LATE
# WITH MY MOTION
## *(Hon. Kenneth Chotiner, Los Angeles)*

THE COURT   Although Defense Counsel admits fault in not filing the written notice of motion, he points out that the fault is not all his own. It was because he was delayed, missed his client in Riverside, and was arrested and charged as a felon in Chino, resulting in stress and the failure to file the motion papers herein demanded by the People.


# WHY THE DA
# DOESN'T WANT TWO JURORS
## *(Bob Boyce, San Diego)*

DA   I would like to indicate some of the reasons for my personal challenges on those two prospective jurors. Mr. A. came in here. He is single. He works at the waste treatment plant, in which I have knowledge because I have prosecuted a good number of the individuals who work there in an undercover drug deal. It came to my attention when I was prosecuting those individuals that there might be a good reason why the San Diego sewer system doesn't work very well because most of the individuals working there were high as kites on most days.

As to Mr. B. . . .

COUNSEL   I don't think he worked at the waste treatment plant.

DA   No, he didn't, but he knew ten individuals who had been, quote, "shot," and he used the word "shot" rather than "killed." There is a significant difference between the two, and one who indicates that his friends have been shot and not killed gives me a certain impression of that individual's thinking.

He also has a haircut that is almost precisely the same haircut as what the defendant had at the time of his arrest. His hair, for the record, is flat on the top; the back portion has a triangular level cutting at the back that is very popular with young people today.

COUNSEL   Mainly blacks.

DA   Since I go to a hairdresser who does that, I have seen her write initials the same way as with black people. It's a very popular style with the flat top and the triangular level. One of the issues here is identification in this particular case.

THE COURT  Are you afraid the witnesses are going to I.D. a juror?

COUNSEL  Maybe we should have a lineup.

DA  Well, I don't know. They might I.D. the defense attorney.

COUNSEL  Judge, while she's looking for her notes. Do you know the attorney Doug Doe?

THE COURT  The name is familiar.

COUNSEL  He's a black attorney. I was in a drug trial over there about eight or nine years ago in Federal Court where he was identified by the witness as the black drug dealer.

DA  As to Mr. B., when he first began to talk, as the record will indicate, he has extremely poor grammar. He, at that point, led me to believe that he might be illiterate because of the syntax he was using.

COUNSEL  Maybe we should give all the jurors a spelling test.

DA  I would love to.

THE COURT  I was thinking of my father-in-law who was a county attorney, which is the equivalent of a district attorney in Arizona, and grew up in Oklahoma, and he speaks differently than he writes.

DA  Well, as Your Honor will not allow us to use jury questionnaires, I have no idea how this person would write. But even when he came back into chambers, his speech is very slow. He not only seemed to be very deliberate in his answers, but his speech pattern was such that he was not as quick or rapid in response as the other jurors have indicated.

When he first referred to the police, he cut the syllable, with "P-O" being emphasized and "L-I-C-E" at the end. On the numerous ride-alongs that I have been involved in, the word "po-lice" is not used in a particularly friendly manner. When he indicated that he had friends and relatives shot, he also indicated that there were approximately ten individuals that he knew who were accused of shooting. Again, he did not use the word "killed."

He indicated that he felt that police had to meet quotas in making arrests. He did not indicate that this was something along the lines of traffic tickets. And that the police didn't always have the facts when they bring someone in on, quote, "technicalities."

He had a relative in Washington, D.C., that was shot by the police.

And one of the first questions that Your Honor asked of this individual when he came back into chambers in regards to the shooting was, "Were any of these people killed by the San Diego Police Department?" which offended me that the

Court would think that the San Diego police had something to do with shooting them as the first question, and I didn't want to place that into his mind, as well.

He also was late. Other than that, he was great.

## IT'S CRYING TIME
### *(Lynda Romero, San Diego)*

**DEFENSE COUNSEL**　Finally, Your Honor, because this is such a highly emotional case, I would ask the Court to admonish Counsel, the district attorney, to refrain from breaking into tears in front of the jury. I mean, this may sound like a frivolous motion, but I'm very serious about this. It has a high emotional impact on the jury.

**THE COURT**　At what stage? Including argument?

**COUNSEL**　At any portion. I can never tell with this prosecutor. I don't know if she's going to break into crying or not. But I would ask her to try to refrain from breaking into tears in front of the jurors, so that won't add more flames to an already very prejudicial situation.

**THE COURT**　This Court has no right to tell Defense Counsel or the prosecutor not to be emotionally involved with his case or her case. That's not proper. That's not up to this Court. I have seen Defense Counsel break down before the jury. I mean, am I going to tell Defense Counsel, don't cry? Don't raise your voice in closing argument? Same thing with the prosecutor. You have a right to do that. If you have an authority along that line, you let me know. I heard one case that Cindy gave me the other day about this prosecutor who was making a lot of noise during the trial.

**DA**        Was he flatulent?

**The Court**        He was passing gas.

**DA**        He was flatulent.

**The Court**        It was reported. And I understand that the case is on appeal, or a motion for new trial. That, I can understand. I mean, that's disgusting. It's completely irresponsible conduct. On the other hand, if the prosecutor is honestly involved in the case, or Defense Counsel is honestly involved in the case, representing your cause, and becoming emotional, I don't see anything wrong with it. Personally, I don't. Because, you know, the courtroom is a very emotionally charged setting.

The defendant has a right to get up there and cry. I cannot tell the defendant, don't cry. The defendant has a right to sit at counsel table and cry. Witnesses have a right to get up here and cry. They do it all the time.

COUNSEL    Judge, the only reason I bring this up, and not to disparage the prosecutor, but I've been in court with her when she cried over a traffic citation over a left-hand turn. And, you know, tears are very powerful, and if she's capable of crying over a left turn, I'd hate to see what could happen in a case like this. And I just don't want that to be part of this case.

THE COURT    Is that true?

DA    Your Honor, this is an incredibly sexist colloquy. I cannot believe it. Especially since last week Counsel said that he was going to be bawling in his argument. He's the one who mentioned crying. You know, just to start looking at a woman prosecutor and say she's going to cry, and she cries over left turns, and he's the one who tells me he's going to be crying in his argument, I refuse to make any further comment, except it's extremely sexist.

COUNSEL    It has nothing to do with sex, Your Honor.

THE COURT    I haven't heard such a motion before, and I don't think it is appropriate for this Court to prohibit anyone to do what he or she must do in representing his side. I'm not going to stop you if you start crying during the course of closing argument.

COUNSEL   It will be on the inside, Your Honor.
THE COURT   Inside or outside, be my guest.


## TEARFUL DUTY
### *(Winston Schoonover, Encino, CA)*

Tears have always been considered legitimate argu-
ments before a jury, and while the question has never
arisen out of any such behavior in this court, we know
of no rule or jurisdiction in the court below to check
them. It would appear to be one of the natural rights
of counsel, which no court or constitution could take
away. It is certainly, if no more, a matter of the highest
personal privilege. Indeed, if Counsel has them at com-
mand, it may be seriously questioned whether it is not
his professional duty to shed them whenever proper
occasion arises.

*Ferguson v. Moore*, 98 Tenn. 343, 351–52 (1897), per Wilkes, J.

# 3

# EVIDENCE

*"My dear sir, it is quite impossible for me to take on your case.
. . . You lack the most important piece of evidence . . . (aside)
evidence that you can pay my fee!"*
*HONORÉ DAUMIER,* LAWYERS AND JUSTICE, NO. 20

| | |
|---|---|
| HALDEMAN | *And there'd be some rules of evidence. Aren't there?* |
| DEAN | *There are rules of evidence.* |
| PRESIDENT | *Both evidence, and you have lawyers.* |
| HALDEMAN | *So you are in a hell of a lot better position than you are up there [before the Committee].* |
| DEAN | *No, you can't have a lawyer before a grand jury.* |
| PRESIDENT | *Oh, no. That's right.* |
| DEAN | *You just can't have a lawyer before a grand jury.* |
| HALDEMAN | *Okay, but you do have rules of evidence. You can refuse to talk.* |
| DEAN | *You can take the Fifth Amendment.* |
| PRESIDENT | *That's right. That's right.* |
| HALDEMAN | *You can say you forgot, too, can't you?* |
| PRESIDENT | *That's right.* |
| DEAN | *But you can't . . . you're in a very high risk perjury situation.* |
| PRESIDENT | *That's right. Just be damned sure you say I don't remember. I can't recall. I can't give any honest . . . answer that I can recall. But that's it.* |

From the Watergate Tapes.

"And during this period, even though you were, in fact, the defendant's best friend, you received nothing from him but an occasional biscuit and a pat on the head?"

## KEEP TO THE SUBJECT
*(Jon Sands, Phoenix, AZ)*

THE COURT  We're not arguing truth here, we're arguing evidence.


## WERE YOU PRESENT WHEN YOUR PICTURE WAS TAKEN?
*(Catherine Ankenbrandt, Baraboo, WI)*

Q. Is Exhibit No. 2 a picture?

A. Yes.

Q. And who is it a picture of?

A. Me.

Q. Can you tell me what you see, or what is Exhibit No. 2?

A. It's a cut to the side of the throat.

Q. Okay. But, before we get to that point, what is this?

A. Me.

Q.  That's not you in person, is it?
A.  Yes.
Q.  And were you present when this picture was taken?
A.  Yes.

## WHO'S LISTENING
(G. Fred Metos, Salt Lake City)

THE COURT    Counsel, could I interrupt you so we can get those exhibits to the jury and have them looking at them while you're examining him, with the caution that they are to pay attention to the testimony, too?

COUNSEL    No, they don't even have to pay attention to the testimony.

DA    No objection.

COUNSEL    It's mostly for my benefit.

THE COURT    Well, that's good. I wasn't listening either.

## PENALTIES OF A SHELTERED LIFE
(Earl Bute, New York City)

Police report: Suspect approached victim from behind, pointed a handgun in the direction of victim, and stated, "Give me the keys to your car, this is a

211." Victim looked toward suspect and asked, "What's a 211?"

## GIVE ME AN EXAMPLE*
*(Patrick Grady, Cedar Rapids)*

THE COURT  Counsel, can you direct me to what evidence there is of prior threats from the victim to the defendant or prior general bad treatment of the victim toward the defendant? I can find nothing in evidence.

COUNSEL  Well, "fuck you."

THE COURT  "Fuck you." I do not consider that to be a threat.

## THE ENVELOPE, PLEASE
*(Danny Fabricant, Ventura, CA)*

THE COURT  I have a document, an envelope within which were contained two envelopes. I have now separated them. They are from the custodian of records of the Los Angeles Police Department. I cannot discern any difference between the two documents. Is there any objection to my opening these to see what they are and then move from there?

DA    Not at all.

Mr. F.    None, Your Honor.

The Court    Within the first packet—first packet says, "We have no records."

Mr. F.    What does the second packet say?

The Court    "See the first packet."

## CHEAP BLOND
### (Michael Watkins, Hillsboro, OR)

Prosecutor    Could you point to someone in this courtroom, or maybe yourself, to indicate exactly how close to a hair color you are referring to?

Witness    Well, something like her's (pointing to Counsel) except for more—The woman right here in front (pointing to Counsel). Except for more cheap bleached-blond hair.

Prosecutor    May the record reflect, Your Honor, the witness has identified Defense Counsel as the cheap blonde.

## EXPERT TESTIMONY
### (Peggy Blanchard, Los Angeles)

Q.    Showing you what's been marked as People's No. 1 for identification, you

Q. testified that was the body you observed at the autopsy; is that right?

A. That is correct.

Q. Can you describe exactly what you saw, what you observed about the body?

A. At the autopsy itself?

Q. Did you observe whether the body was alive or appeared to be deceased?

A. Deceased.

Q. And what makes you draw that conclusion? Describe exactly what you saw.

COUNSEL Your Honor, I would be willing to stipulate if there was an autopsy being performed on the body, that the body—that person was no longer alive.

THE COURT We certainly hope so.


## EXCITING DIALOGUE
*(Anonymous Bosch, Paris, ID)*

COUNSEL (for the Department) We concede "A," "B," and "C" are too late.

THE COURT "A," "B," and "C" are too late?

COUNSEL Yes, sir.

THE COURT Anything else? So are we concerned about "D"—"F," "G"—we are concerned about "D," "E," "F"—

COUNSEL "D" is a summary of "A," "B," and "C."

THE COURT    We are concerned about "E," "F," "G,"
             and "H"?

COUNSEL      Forget "F." Just "E," "G"—just "E"
             and "G." "H" is a summary of "G."

From *Dept. of Revenue v. Sobieralski*, 92 Ill. App. 3d 925 (1981)

## READ ONLY
### *(Anonymous Bosch, Paris, ID)*

Q.    Can you tell the jury what you did in
      reference to the Department of Motor
      Vehicles?

A.    Well, I made a number of inquiries,
      principally by computer, to identify who
      rented the beeper.

COUNSEL    I would object to the contents of
           computer response as being hearsay.

THE COURT    Shall we bring it in to cross-examine it?

## KINSEY REPORT*
### *(Regina Zupan, Boston)*

PROSECUTOR    Exactly what did he do concerning the
              anal sex?

A.    He started to, took himself and started
      to have anal sex.

PROSECUTOR    How did that feel? Describe the pain.

DEFENSE COUNSEL    Your Honor, may we approach side bar.
                   (Conference at side bar.)

| | |
|---|---|
| DEFENSE COUNSEL | Your Honor, this is not a civil case, we are not going for emotional distress. |
| THE COURT | Well, it has to do with her state of mind. |
| DEFENSE COUNSEL | In terms of? |
| THE COURT | In terms of whether it is consensual. |
| PROSECUTOR | The jury may well infer that no one would consent to that sort of pain. |
| THE COURT | I'll allow it. |
| DEFENSE COUNSEL | A lot of people do practice anal sex. |
| PROSECUTOR | I am not acquainted with them. |

## NOW IT CAN BE TOLD: WRESTLING IS FAKE
*(Paul Morris, Coral Gables)*

| | |
|---|---|
| COUNSEL | And between 1980 and 1989, where did you live? |
| DEFENDANT | I was working and I moved to California and I moved to Puerto Rico and I started working Puerto Rico as a professional wrestler. |
| Q. | Is that like Olympic wrestling? |
| A. | No, like World Wrestling Federation. |
| Q. | And how long were you a wrestler? |
| A. | Four years and a half. |
| Q. | Let me ask you one question I have always wanted to know. Is that real wrestling? |
| A. | It's real for us, you know. We know how |

|  |  |
|---|---|
|  | to do it. If you get into it, you get hurt, but it's fake. We know who is going to win before. |
| PROSECUTOR | I object, Your Honor. |
| THE COURT | Do I ask you the basis? |
| PROSECUTOR | I withdraw the objection. |
| DEFENSE COUNSEL | Would you like to demonstrate the sleeper hold on the prosecutor? |
| DEFENDANT | If he wants me to, I will show it to him. |

## PURSED LIPS
*(Kate Thickstun, San Diego)*

|  |  |
|---|---|
| Q. | N-1, your number, that is a DEA exhibit number, is this the purse the methamphetamine was contained in? |
| A. | Yes, sir. |
| Q. | What else was in the purse, do you recall, besides the methamphetamine? |
| THE COURT | We are not trying the criminal case. We know that the methamphetamine was there. No one contests that, right? |
| COUNSEL | No, we don't contest that. |
| THE COURT | All right. |
| COUNSEL | I would like to know what else, if anything, was in there so I can determine where all these other items were when they conducted the second search. |
| THE COURT | This is not a criminal trial. All we are doing is sentencing right now. |

Counsel     I understand.
The Court   If we have to go through everything that
            is in a woman's purse we will be here for
            a month . . . Don't tell that to my wife.


## NOBODY DOES DEBBIE*
*(Michael L. Harris, Kansas City)*

Q.  You admitted that you've had sex with
    some of the people there. Did you have
    sex with Debbie?

A.  No.

Q.  You never had any sex with her?

Q.  Have you ever had oral sex with her?

A.  No.

Q.  You did not say down in Coffeyville that
    you told everybody you had oral sex with
    Debbie?

A.  With Debbie? No, man, you don't admit
    that. No. Even if you did, you wouldn't
    admit it. No, sir. No, sir. No. On the
    record, no. No, sir.

Q.  All right.

A.  Man.

## EYEWITNESS
*(Barry Newman, Dixon, CA)*

COUNSEL    Do you now wear corrective glasses?
WITNESS    There are three of you?
COUNSEL    No. There's only one of me.


## THE REMARKABLE
## SHRINKING WITNESS*
*(Michael Roman, Berkeley)*

Q.    Do you recall any identifying features like scars, moles, anything like that, not looking at him now, but what you remember that evening?

A.    I remember he was so skinny it looked like his eyes were too big for his face, that if he sneezed too hard or farted too loud his bones would pop out of his skin.

DEFENDANT    I'm ready to whip this bitch now. Going to get her ass whipped.

COUNSEL    (to Defendant) This man is taking down everything you say. It can come back in a jury trial. (To Witness) How tall would you say this person was?

A.    Tall.

Q.    How tall are you?

A.    During the summer 5'2", during the winter I'm 5'1".

Q.    This was winter time?

A.    February.

Q.    You were 5'1" at that time?

A.    Okay.

THE COURT    How you do that?

WITNESS    I don't know, Judge, it just happens.

THE COURT    That's remarkable.

WITNESS    I know.

## THE LOONEY KIN
### (Lair Franklin, Los Angeles)

THE COURT    Well, there is Spooky, Smiley, Sleepy?

COUNSEL    I don't think there is a Smiley. New Bone?

WITNESS    There is a Smiley, too.

DA    I meant to say with Spooky?

WITNESS    Yes.

THE COURT    Yes. Was Droopy there?

WITNESS    No, Droopy was at the store. He was there, though.

THE COURT    I accept that.

DA    What is your nickname?

WITNESS    Looney.

DA    Looney. No further questions.

## JUDICIAL RULING
*(Roy Dahlberg, Sacramento)*

| | |
|---|---|
| DA | Objection, Your Honor, calls for speculation. |
| THE COURT | Overruled, unless you can qualify it as to her having been told. |
| COUNSEL | You mean sustained, Your Honor? |
| THE COURT | Pardon? |
| COUNSEL | Did you mean objection sustained or overruled? |
| THE COURT | I'm sorry. If I said sustained, I meant—overruled, I meant sustained, unless— |
| COUNSEL | Thank you. I'll rephrase the question. |

## MISDIRECTION
*(Hayes Gable, Sacramento)*

| | |
|---|---|
| WITNESS | I can picture going back this way. (Indicating) |
| COUNSEL | Let the record reflect what direction—what the witness pointed to. |
| THE COURT | To her right. |
| COUNSEL | Which would be west. |
| THE COURT | Well— |
| COUNSEL | Wouldn't it? |
| THE COURT | You mean really west? |
| COUNSEL | From here, that's the way she pointed. I think she's pointing east, if she's facing the west. |

| | |
|---|---|
| THE COURT | She is pointing west, pointing toward the railroad yards. |
| COUNSEL | In relation to this map, she pointed east. |
| THE COURT | I said "really" where she is pointing. That is west. On the diagram—she is pointing east on the diagram. |

## SAY WHAT?
*(J.J. Paul, Indianapolis)*

| | |
|---|---|
| DA | Do you know Raymond? |
| COUNSEL | Your Honor, I'm gonna object on this basis, this is certainly outside the scope of the direct examination. |
| PROSECUTOR | Your Honor, these questions are preliminary to the manner for which the questions are designed for relevance and scope. |
| THE COURT | For what? |
| PROSECUTOR | If the Court, if the Court will allow me to proceed. |
| THE COURT | I'm afraid I don't follow you. |
| PROSECUTOR | Now the questions are, the questions are not outside the scope of direct examination, Your Honor, because it's, they're merely a preliminary foundation questions to direct this witness to the substance of that testimony that was referred to, although not referred to by name. |

COUNSEL    Same objection, Your Honor.
THE COURT  The objection is sustained.


## STOLEN SEEDS*
*(Edward F. Novak, Phoenix, AZ)*

Q. To this day you deny paternity, don't
   you?
A. I don't deny paternity. I've acknowledged
   the child and I admitted it judicially in a
   pleading.
Q. How is it possible that you could be the
   father of this child without having had
   sexual contact with the mother?
A. There are a number of ways. One is
   artificial insemination.
Q. Did that happen in this case?
A. I don't know.
Q. You don't know whether artificial
   insemination happened?
A. That's correct.
Q. Are you a donor at a sperm bank here in
   town?
A. No, I'm not a donor.
Q. How would she artificially inseminate
   herself with your sperm?
A. I'm not quite certain if it even did
   occur, but there was the possibility of it
   occurring.
Q. How would she get ahold of your sperm?

A. She cleaned my office on several occasions, and there was refrigerated sperm in the refrigerator during that period of time.

Q. So your theory is, she got into your refrigerator and inseminated herself with your sperm. That's your testimony?

COUNSEL Object to Counsel's manner of asking the question—laughing.

Q. I'm not trying to be facetious. Is that your testimony?

A. I don't have any theory. You're asking how it's possible and that's what I told you.

Q. What would the other things be?

A. I told you that I don't recall having any sexual contact with her and that's the truth. I don't have any recollection of it. If this could occur at a time when I was comatose, that's a possibility.

Q. Were you comatose in February or March?

A. There was a period of time when I was under very heavy sedation for what has really never been truly diagnosed, but something that kept me from being able to walk.

Q. And you were sedated and she had access to your body? So that's a possibility? She may have what—raped you without your knowledge? Is that what you're telling us?

A. I don't know if you want a technical

definition of rape. I'm guessing. If, in fact, the child is mine, that's another possible way it happened.

Q. That she had sex with you without your knowledge?

A. Without me being aware of it, correct.


## WEDDING BELLS & SYMBOLS*
*(Dan Fiduccia, San Jose)*

Q. Is this the invitation that you saw before you went to the wedding?

A. Yes, it is.

Q. What is it that appears to you to be on the cover of this invitation?

A. I thought it's just a simple design.

Q. On the cover of this invitation there appears to be some sort of a whip?

A. Yes, now that you mention it, yes. But what we have at home are different than this.

# 4

# THE EXPERTS

*"An expert is one who knows more and more about less and less."*

$\qquad$ *NICHOLAS MURRAY BUTLER*

*"It has already been established that the defendant was bothered and bewildered. In your expert opinion, was he also bewitched?"*

## SWITCH HITTER
*(Tom Penfield, San Diego)*

PLAINTIFF'S LAWYER   Is that your conclusion, that this man is a malingerer?

PSYCHIATRIST   I wouldn't be testifying if I didn't think so, unless I was on the other side, then it would be a post-traumatic condition.

From *Ladner v. Higgins*, 71 So. 2d 242, 244 (La. Ct. App. 1954)


## SENSE OF THE EXPERT
*(Peter G. Degelleke, Bedford, MA)*

Q.   What about the research?

A.   I don't think there is any research on that. There's a logical hunch that may be true, but I know of no research study that would support that at this point in time.

Q.   What about just common sense?

A.  Well, I am not here using common sense. I'm here as an expert.


# FORENSIC COMPLAINER
### (Mark Greenberg, Berkeley)

Q.  Doctor, you didn't do any objective testing?

A.  No.

Q.  No Rorschach, no MMPI?

A.  No.

Q.  No TAT?

A.  No.

Q.  Why not?

A.  I'll tell you very clearly. The Court pays a certain amount of money for this. Let me tell you, I am not making a living from this. I do not make a living from this. For example, in court today, this is the last thing I want to do is spend time here. Nothing against the Court or jurors or anything. I do very well in my practice. Spending time here is costing me a great deal of money. This is not my desire. For this amount of money, I feel I'm doing charity in this type of report. This is a lot of work for what I'm paid. And I don't bill any extra for it, which is really ludicrous.

This business here I can't positively state,

but listening to this taped confession,
reading all this other business for the fee
that I'm paid, I probably didn't submit
another bill, but I should have, and I really
should, but I don't, and the fee is just—I'm
just not going to do it any more.

Jury, you know, maybe you should feel
prejudiced against me because I didn't do
any testing. I don't care. I really don't. I
can't do any more for this price. If
somebody else can do it, God love them.

Q. Thank you.
A. Pleasure.


## DIRECTION EXPERT
*(Andrew Rubin, Santa Monica)*

DEFENSE COUNSEL  Doctor, you testified that the deceased
was shot in the chest by a 12-gauge
shotgun from a distance of not more
than three feet?

WITNESS  Yes.

DEFENSE COUNSEL  And that this caused his immediate
death, is that correct?

WITNESS  Yes.

DEFENSE COUNSEL  Now, Doctor, which way would someone
fall after receiving a 12-gauge shotgun
blast directly in the chest from a distance
of three feet or less?

WITNESS  Down.

## MIXED NEIGHBORHOOD
*(Richard Krech, Oakland)*

Q.  What kind of neighborhood would you describe this area in terms of crime rates and things like that?
A.  Half low-life, half residential.


## COKE EXPERT
*(Charles W.B. Fels, Knoxville, TN)*

A.  We weighed it up and made sure that each unit weighed a kilo and did a general purity test on it.
Q.  How do you do a general purity test?
A.  Well, we snorted a bunch of it.


## MERCHANDISE RETURN
*(Hon. Marvin O. Teague, Austin, TX)*

Q.  You were mentioning something about this Horace. Is that his name? Is it Horace?
A.  Horace.
Q.  Do you know what his last name is?
A.  No.
Q.  And you said he sells bad drugs?
A.  Yes.

Q. Okay. And has he ever sold you bad drugs?

A. Has he ever sold who?

Q. You bad drugs?

A. No.

Q. How do you know that he does that?

A. Because most time he's selling them and people come back up there with a pistol or gun or something and ask for their money back.

## THE MAJESTY OF THE LAW*
*(Andrew Rubin, Santa Monica)*

Q. He had a bowel movement, had he not?

A. I don't know. I was told he had.

Q. You didn't smell it?

DA Excuse me. I am going to move to strike the last statement, the witness lacks personal knowledge.

THE COURT Motion to strike is granted. Ladies and gentlemen, disregard what he was told.

Q. Did you smell anything that would lead you to the opinion that Mr. F. had had a bowel movement in his pants?

A. Yes, I did.

Q. What did you smell?

A. Smelled like—smelled like crap.

DA I am going to object and ask the Court to strike the answer. Even though he can

testify as to what he smelled, he can't
testify that it was the defendant's
because there is no feces test, and in
that sense it lacks foundation.

THE COURT    It would go to the weight of it.


## DEAD TOOTH EXPERT
*(Quin Denvir, Sacramento)*

Q. How do you know these teeth came from
a dead man, by the way?
A. How do I know that the teeth I
examined came from a dead man?
Q. Yes.
A. Because they weren't moving.


## SEX EXPERT*
*(Grace Suarez, San Francisco)*

Q. And what was the defendant doing at
that time?
A. He was engaged in a sex act of sexual
intercourse with a female.
Q. How do you know that?
A. I was in vice for three and a half years
and I just left vice and come back to
uniform.

## BLIND STUDY EXPERT
*(Delgado Smith, Texarkana, TX)*

THE COURT   Would you explain to the jury what a double-blind study is.

WITNESS   It's always prospective. That means you plan your study ahead of time; you don't take data from the past, and you do something to one group and you don't do it to the other group, and the examiners don't know which group—the examiners don't know which group is the study group and which group is the control group to whom that has not been done; and the only way I could conceive of doing that in this population is to do—as I suggested—to molest ten and not the other ten and have the examiners be double-blinded.

## HARD-ASS EXPERT*
*(Delgado Smith, Texarkana, TX)*

Q.   How long would it take for a sphincter spasm to heal, Doctor?

A.   Sphincter spasm is not a disease process. I mean, as you stand there, you can have sphincter spasm if you wanted to.

Q.   I could have a sphincter spasm right now if I wanted to?

A.   Just tighten your sphincter and that is your sphincter spasm. Try it.

Q.   Can you have one right now, Doctor?

A.   Yeah, I think we all can.

## GENE EXPERT
*(James Farley, Ventura, CA)*

Q.   How do the conclusions of Doctor C. fit into what you just said about people leaving their genes where they go?

A.   Well, one of the reasons that I was interested in the paper was that it did show gene flow into and out of these small isolated populations. And I haven't read the paper for many years, but my recollection is of a swarthy stranger coming in and spreading his genes wherever he could, for want of a better term.

And so I found that this field was a really exciting field to enter into because it was an academically approved way of thinking about sex all the time. So I said, this is the field for me. This is good.

COUNSEL A.   May I remove my jacket, Your Honor?

THE COURT   Sure.

COUNSEL B.   Leave your genes on.

WITNESS   That's how you can tell a boy chromosome from a girl chromosome. Pull down their genes.

## EQUAL OPPORTUNITY
*(James Lingle, Rogers, AR)*

THE COURT   Well, I'd be interested in such testimony. I think I could take judicial notice that that's not true, but I'd be glad to hear it and, you know, make up my mind. I was born and grew up in South Arkansas. I think I know how things work. I don't believe I need any Ph.D. to tell me. But if you want to call him or her, I won't turn it off. I find experts almost always unhelpful.

COUNSEL   I think I would like to call him, in that case, Your Honor.

THE COURT   Since I find them unhelpful?

COUNSEL   Well, no, Your Honor, but if they're calling unhelpful experts, I'd better call unhelpful experts.

## CASE STINKS
*(Kenneth Quigley, San Francisco)*

Q.   Did you seize those shoes?

A.   Pardon me.

Q.   Did you seize the shoes?

A.   I impounded the shoes, yes.

Q.   Did you bring them to court? Yes?

A.   I have the . . . I'm sorry, you have them.

DA    Showing Counsel a brown sealed paper bag, we'd ask the Court to have it marked People's 1 for identification. Ask for a pair of scissors, if I could, please. Now opening the bag by cutting it across the side. Showing Counsel the contents. They are without Odor-Eaters. (Visibly gagging)

DA    May I approach, Judge?

THE COURT    Certainly.

DA    They are without Odor-Eaters. May the contents be marked as People's 1-A, collectively, pair of black Adidas shoes?

THE COURT    1-A.

DA    Deputy, would you take a look at the shoes? Are these the shoes you just talked about?

A.    Without getting too close, yes, they are.


## IDENTIFICATION EXPERT
*(Robert Friedman, San Bernardino)*

Q.    Deputy, showing you photographs numbers 3 and 4, can you identify those?

A.    Those were photographs taken at our sheriff's headquarters.

Q.    Do you recognize the individuals in the photographs?

A.    Yes, sir.

Q.    And, in Exhibit No. 3, do you recognize that subject?

A. Yes, sir.

Q. How do you recognize him?

A. There's a name card in front of him.
(Whereupon, the Court broke into
laughter.)

THE COURT Oh, I love that. We don't get paid
much, but we do have a good time.

## LAB EXPERT
### (Jim Pokorny, San Diego)

Q. My last couple questions, is it true that
your laboratory for which you work is
jokingly known as "Malfunction
Junction"?

A. It is?

Q. I am asking you.

A. I have not heard it. They have more
sense than to say it to my face.

Q. Was there not a sign on your door that
said for a long time "Malfunction
Junction"?

A. How do you know these things?

Q. Here's a picture of your front door,
right?

A. I'll be damned. Okay. That's been gone
for at least a year.

Q. When you said earlier that I wasn't
known as that—

A. I forgot.

Q. That wasn't true?

A. I forgot. What is truth? It was taken off the door. Could I see that door? I don't even think it is in the present laboratory.

Q. It was taken off the door right after I took this picture.

A. Oh, is that when it was taken off?

Q. Yes. The flash woke somebody up in there.

A. Well, somebody has a strange sense of humor. It says: "Nothing works here." That's nasty.

Q. Take a look at that photograph which I have put on the board. Is that a photograph of the insides of this machine with the oven lid removed?

A. Yes.

Q. Would you show us where this column is that you passed out a diagram of?

A. It is this thing that goes up and around.

Q. That backup tubing there?

A. Yes.

Q. That's the column?

A. Here's the oven. Do you have the column in here?

Q. That's what I'm asking you. Would a closer view assist you?

A. This isn't a trick question, is it? The column is there, right?

Q. This is the column.

A. That's what I said.

Q. Then you didn't seem to be sure.

A. It is in color. I am not used to color photographs.

Q. It is in color in real life, isn't it?

A. No, actually. This is beautiful photography, and when you look at it, you don't see this type of coloring.

## TAUTOLOGY
### *(Kyle Gee, Oakland)*

Q. Prior to that time he used the cocaine?

A. He has always been an up sort of guy. He was wired, yeah. I got a little saying with cocaine. The first thing cocaine makes you feel is like a new person. The first thing a new person wants is cocaine.

## EXPERT TESTIMONY
### *(Anonymous Bosch, Florence, ID)*

Q. Officer, have you ever cut yourself?

A. Yes, sir.

Q. When you cut yourself, did something come out?

A. Yes, sir.

Q. What color was that?

COUNSEL  I object, Your Honor, as irrelevant.

THE COURT  Overruled.

WITNESS  It was red.

Q. Did that red substance that came out appear to be similar to the red substance you saw at the scene?

A. Yes, sir.

Q. Does that red substance have a name?

A. Yes, sir, it does.

Q. What is it called?

A. Blood.

# 5

# THE JUDGES

"One wills at the beginning the result; one finds the principle afterwards; such is the genesis of all juridical construction."

*SALEILLES*

"The judge becomes an enemy of the accused, of a chained man, prey to the horrors of squalor, torture, and a most terrible future, he does not look for the truth of the fact but for the crime in the prisoner; he lays snares for him and, if they fail, believes he has personally lost something and has undermined the sense of infallibility which man arrogates to himself in all things. The judge has the power to decide what inquiries suffice for imprisonment; in order that a person may prove himself innocent he must first be declared guilty. This is what is called an offensive prosecution—the typical form of criminal procedure in almost every part of enlightened Europe in the eighteenth century."

*BECCARIA*

"Associate [U.S. Supreme Court] Justice William McReynolds [was so] incredibly anti-Semitic that he avoided speaking to [Justice] Brandeis for a three-year period, refused to sit next to him in the annual Court picture for 1924 (hence no picture was taken that year), and on one occasion wrote to Chief Justice Taft, 'As you know I am not always to be found when there is a Hebrew aboard. . . .'"

*BRUCE ALLEN MURPHY*, THE
BRANDEIS/FRANKFURTER CONNECTION

*"Well,* recuse *me!"*

# JUDICIAL OVERREACHING

*Occasionally, judges do things they shouldn't and are called to the Bar to explain. In* Matter of Deming, 736 P.2d 639 (1987), *the judge's clerks testified as follows:*

Q.  I wonder if you could describe to the Commission exactly what he did?

A.  He came out to my desk and he told me to stand up, he wanted to give me a hug and he gave me a hug, and when he did that, he reached up very quickly and he unlatched my bra strap.

Q.  After he unlatched your bra strap, did he make a comment to you?

A.  He said something to the effect of, "Gee, I haven't lost my touch."

*And another testified:*

Q.  In the summer of 1985 was there an incident that took place in his assistant's office?

A.  Yes. He would ask me if it was okay if
he touched me and I would—I think I
said no and he kind of chased me
around his clerk's desk. He ended up
jumping over the top of one of them to
touch me. . . .

*And another said:*

Q.  Was there ever an occasion in
connection with your duties . . . that you
felt that Judge Deming acted toward you
in an improper manner?

A.  There was. When I was back in
chambers one time trying to get
information from Lettie, Judge Deming
came back and asked me if I would
come into his chambers and take my
clothes off and bend over.

# UT PUTO ET DEO
## *(N. Reese Bagwell, Clarksville, TN)*

THE COURT   All right. I sure would feel better if you
had a lawyer. You can afford one, can't
you?

DEFENDANT   No, I can't, Your Honor. I cannot afford
an attorney.

THE COURT   Are you drawing your salary from the fire
department?

DEFENDANT   Yes, I am.

| THE COURT | That is a pretty good salary, isn't it? I mean by that, firemen get paid pretty well. |
| DEFENDANT | Well, it is not comparable to yours, but it is decent. |
| THE COURT | Well, it ought not to be comparable to mine. I mean, after all, we are the highest in the State. We are God. |

## SAY THE SECRET WORD
*(Anthony Polvino, Portland, OR)*

| Q. | You indicated at the time you seized it, it had damage to the dashboard? |
| A. | That's correct. |
| Q. | And one of the windows? |
| A. | That's correct. |
| Q. | Do you yourself know what happened? |
| PROSECUTOR | Again, I believe that is an area—he is going into an area you already ruled upon. |
| DEFENSE COUNSEL | The last time they had it, it got damaged. |
| THE COURT | I have not heard any words of magic, have you, Virgil? |
| COURT REPORTER | No, I haven't. |
| PROSECUTOR | You mean, I should say I object? |
| THE COURT | That's the one. |
| PROSECUTOR | Excuse me. |
| THE COURT | That brings the rubber duck down. |

PROSECUTOR  Objection.
THE COURT  Sustained.

## NOW HEAR THIS
*(Martin Blake, Torrance, CA)*

COUNSEL  May I interrupt for a moment? There seems to be a member of our audience who is mouthing obscenities at our witness and other things, and I would like that she be admonished.
THE COURT  All obscenities must be directed to the Court. You may proceed.
COUNSEL  Thank you, Your Honor.

## AND JUST WHAT IS HEARSAY?
*(Lawrence Weber, Van Nuys, CA)*

Q.  Did the mother tell you that the child had been lying to her?
COUNSEL  Objection. Hearsay.
THE COURT  I will sustain the objection. Just tell us what she said to you.

## ON THE NOD
### (Gerry Sevier, Visalia, CA)

COUNSEL    It's innocuous that somebody drops their
head down and picks it back up in the
bar; the person could have been yawning,
doing anything there in the bar. This
officer didn't know if she was drunk.
Didn't know if she was a danger to
herself. She was sitting down at a table.
I mean, my God, what can a person do
in the bar if they can't drop their head
down for a split second and pick it up?
You can do that on the job. You can do
it while you're in court sometimes. You
can be sitting here at the bench and be
totally bored with what I have to say for
a minute.

THE COURT  I am going to drop my head right now.


## THERE GOES
## THE NEIGHBORHOOD
### (Danny Fabricant, Ventura, CA)

DEFENDANT  You know, I hate coming out here at
seven in the morning and having to sit
downstairs with a bunch of criminals.

THE COURT  I have to do the same thing every day.

DEFENDANT  Yeah, but you don't have to sit down in
a holding tank with 'em.

THE COURT     Every day I come in and I meet the
              dregs of society, and then I have to meet
              their clients. Think of that.


## BADMOUTHING*
### (Jack Schwartz, Los Angeles)

THE COURT     All right. Let's go on the record. Outside
              the presence of the jury right now,
              Counsel and I have had a meeting on
              jury instructions in chambers. And there
              was an objection by the defense and the
              Court has sustained that on the basis
              that that instruction uses the term
              "person using a deadly weapon." And
              this Court has no authority for the
              proposition that the mouth as a general
              proposition is a deadly weapon, and no
              evidence that the defendant has been
              trained in the marital arts or some other
              form of arts so that he knows how to
              use his mouth as a deadly weapon. And
              based on that fact, the Court will sustain
              the objection.

## JUDICIAL DISTEMPER
*(Renee Captor, Syracuse, NY)*

MR. M.   Sir, I want to get clarification.

THE COURT   Clarification is you can't—you park legal. I will give you a break on the other one. You don't fill up a handicapped zone; do you understand me? Is it clear to you?

MR. M.   Sure.

THE COURT   Otherwise, if you want to park in a handicapped spot, I will come over and break your leg for you so you can use it legally.

MR. M.   Is that a threat, sir?

THE COURT   Next time you come in this Court and make that kind of noise, you son-of-a-bitch, I will send you to jail, you got it?

MR. M.   Yes.

THE COURT   Keep that mouth of yours shut or I will come in there myself and strangle you, you bastard. Get out of here.

## COURT ORDER I
*(Judy Clarke, San Diego)*

Defendant's oral motion to cut, dye, and perm hair—granted as to rinse/dye. Denied as to permanent.

## COURT ORDER: RECUSAL
### (S. Lee Ruslander, Westchester, PA)

Comes now the Judge, and, feeling that the ravishing pits of Hell are too good for this son-of-a-bitch, disqualifies himself from further proceedings in this case.


## INCOMPATIBLE*
### (Seymour Applebaum, Santa Monica)

DA    Well, to use the vernacular, I've been screwed by judges when I assumed that—

THE COURT    Mr. DA, you're not my type, so don't worry about it.

DA    Thank you, Your Honor.


## JOE WHO?
### (David Bukey, Seattle)

THE COURT    Well, I have no power to do anything about that. We either go to trial today or we grant a continuance and set a new trial date and determine what should be the terms pending the trial. We need to first of all clarify who your lawyer is. Who is your lawyer?

DEFENDANT    Do I have to expose him?

THE COURT    Well, certainly.
DEFENDANT    Jehovah.
THE COURT    Joe who?
DEFENDANT    Jehovah.
THE COURT    Is he a member of the Washington State Bar Association?


## AMEN★
*(David Rawson, Bakersfield, CA)*

Q.    Now, do you recall telling Officer F. that after David went into the living room that Gary assumed a missionary position, on top of you?
A.    Yes.
THE COURT    Excuse me, Counsel. What kind of position?
MR. J.    A missionary position, on top of—
THE COURT    Like in prayer?


## ONE WILD AND CRAZY KIND OF GUY
*(Richard Krech, Oakland)*

DEFENDANT    I have no faith in Mr. G. and I don't—I'm sure his word is good, but I hate to say it but I feel Mr. G. might be approaching senility.

THE COURT   Now Mr. G. is an expert defense lawyer. I have tried cases against him, I have had cases in my courtroom with him, I have watched him over the years. He's a former Assistant Public Defender. Contrary to your opinion, he is not senile. He's always acted that way.

## THE SUBPOENA*
*(Stephen Hauser, Santa Monica)*

DA   What happened next, ma'am?

WITNESS   He unzipped his pants and pulled out his subpoena.

THE COURT   Any motions, Counsel?

MR. K.   I move to dismiss, Your Honor. All my client did was pull out a subpoena. There's no law against that.

THE COURT   Counsel, if the witness doesn't know the difference between a penis and a subpoena, that's her problem. Held to answer!

## SHOT DOWN
*(Hon. Paul Turner, Los Angeles)*

THE COURT   I am going to set aside the default. I will give you an opportunity to answer within thirty days, provided you pay to the attorney and to the plaintiff the sum of $10,000 as a condition for the efforts that they have put in to date.

MR. B.   Your Honor, could I ask under what statute you are relying in setting aside the default? Is it under 473?

THE COURT   I can do it under either one or both, and I am doing it under both. I think it should be tried on the merits.

MR. B.   With respect to the lateness of the documents, just for the record, the documents were timely filed. The Court requested the exhibits be removed—

THE COURT   I am not arguing with you on it. I told you—some day I am going to come off this bench and return to my younger days, and I am going to boot people in the you-know-what. Because I don't care if either one or both of you win this case. I have shot and killed better men than both of you, I have. And the only reason I did it on that day is they had a different color shirt than I did. I was wearing gray and the Japanese had a different color on. I had nothing against them.

Now, every time somebody rules in here—and this is the third time today—somebody throws their nose up and goes sideways. I agree with all of you, and I am not going to try it. Common courtesy dictates that a professional—if you want to appeal, run a writ. Out of the kindness of my heart I tell you that I met your man and took your papers, and I had a chance to read them. If you don't like that, then I didn't meet your man and I didn't read it. Okay?

MR. B.     Fine, Your Honor.

THE COURT     But just back off, both of you. All of you back off the courts.

MR. B.     Thank you.


## JUDGE SPEAKS HIS MIND
*(Harry Reinhart, Columbus, OH)*

THE COURT     All right. Once again, I hate arguing against the courts, because that's what it seems like I have to do sometimes. I've got to find some way to get around some rule that some court has pronounced about something, and I don't think we should have to admittedly—okay. I'm not great on defendants' rights. I just don't see why we bend over backward, because most of the time, if the person was innocent, they wouldn't be in trouble in the first place.

So, why is it that we get in trouble when we've got the guilty guy, but somehow or another we've got to do something to protect them? You know, it is beyond me.

The courts have to have these rules to save the one out of a million, or, you know, whatever it is.

So, you can argue until you're blue in the face. I'll agree with you that it is a close call, but I don't choose on close calls to read it in favor of the defendant. I just don't see that we have to do that. I don't know why we should.

## BUD LITE
*(John Williams, Prescott, AZ)*

THE COURT   Next cause, State of Arizona versus—

BAILIFF   Bud'll be right back.

THE COURT   Where did he go, Harry?

BAILIFF   The restroom.

THE COURT   I will take a short break until Bud gets back.

(Recess)

THE COURT   The record can now reflect the presence of the somewhat lighter State's attorney, the defendant, and his attorney.

## JET STREAM*
*(Kenneth Quigley, San Francisco)*

Q. Did the men who came down the ramp say anything to you before jumping you?

A. No, they did not.

Q. Did you urinate on yourself when you were jumped?

A. No, I did not.

Q. Were you still in the act of urinating when you were jumped?

A. No, I had just finished. Would you like to know what color it was?

A. Yes, please.

THE COURT Wait a minute, wait a minute. Enough smartness. Okay. And move onto something else please. The man has wet the wall.


## THE COLOR OF URINE*
*(Dan Mayfield, San Jose)*

In answer to the defense attorney's argument that a two-year-old urine sample (which had turned brown) would prejudice the jury against the defendant:

THE COURT I'm not sure what is supposed to happen to urine which is not refrigerated and left in a bottle for two years. I mean, I'm not sure whether it's supposed to turn and become dark brown or not.

I know that a good bottle of French Sauterne is bottled and it's pale yellow, and within ten or twenty years it might be a mahogany color, and actually it becomes more valuable, they tell me, at that stage than when it's bottled. But here, of course, we're not talking of wine, we're talking of urine.

Off the record. Why did I say that?

## HAIR TODAY, GONE TOMORROW
### *(Bruce Ratcliffe, Urbana, IL)*

THE COURT   Since the defendant has decided to appear with some mysterious designation on his head, when he shows up at the detention center, see to it that this entire side of his head is shaven, and if there is going to be any problem with that, we will take whatever steps are necessary to see to it that at the detention center we don't have gang markings on our inmates.

COUNSEL   Your Honor, I feel compelled to object to that order. I don't believe that the Court has authority to order a person to get a haircut.

THE COURT   Well, I am not ordering him to get it cut. I am ordering him to take off the gang insignia that he has apparently put on his head.

**DEFENDANT** Sir, this is not a gang.

**THE COURT** What is it?

**DEFENDANT** It's just a part.

**THE COURT** It's a what?

**DEFENDANT** It's a part we put in our hair.

**THE COURT** Well, it strikes me as rather peculiar. I remain skeptical of this, and let me suggest this. This is not my area of expertise. From having seen other observations, I believe it to be as I have indicated, but I will defer to the judgment of others in this field whom I believe to be experts. One of them is Officer X., and you can designate anyone else that you want, Counsel, and if they say this isn't a gang insignia, as I believe it to be, I will authorize the probation officer to simply disregard this order.

**COUNSEL** Regardless of who has expertise, Your Honor, I am not certain that the Court has the authority to order someone's head shaved.

**THE COURT** Well, I am not ordering his head shaved. I am just ordering that portion of his head.

**COUNSEL** I don't think you have the authority to order his head shaved.

**THE COURT** Let me put it this way. I believe the Court has the authority not to permit people—if I am correct, that that's a gang insignia—come into my institution with it on, and that's the basis of my judgment, and my ruling. If I am incorrect, you know the way to go to the Appeals Court.

COUNSEL But, Your Honor, going to the Appeals Court will be quite difficult concerning a haircut, if the Court has ordered it to be before one-thirty tomorrow.

THE COURT Well, that's twenty-four hours. You are telling me I don't have authority, then that's a determination you are going to have to get in writing from some higher court, which would be an indication that the law makes no sense, and is truly an ass.

COUNSEL The First Amendment says you burn a flag as free speech; it seems to me he can have a haircut any way he wants to have.

THE COURT A First Amendment issue—a gang insignia carved into your head?

## ACIDIC EXCHANGE
*(Kent Schaffer, Houston)*

THE COURT Counsel, I am going to ask you that unless you have a throat lozenge, that you not eat candy in the courtroom.

COUNSEL I have Rolaids.

THE COURT    Rolaids?

COUNSEL      Consumes forty-seven times its weight in excess stomach acid, and I have stomach acid.

THE COURT    You create some stomach acid on the part of the Court.

COUNSEL      I have two left.


## MOTION FOR FAIR TRIAL
### (Michael R. Hauptman, Atlanta)

DA           The defendant then walked past him from behind, and I noticed the deputy walking behind him. At that moment, I saw him escorted toward the detention/holding cell area. I had no idea that the deputies were going to take that action. And at that point, I indicated to Defense Counsel that there might be a problem, and the State is not standing in opposition to his motion [for mistrial] here, and I just wanted to . . .

THE COURT    That State's what?

DA           The State's not standing in any opposition to his motion here. So I just . . .

THE COURT    Why aren't you? You're representing the State.

# WITH SYMPATHY,
# BUT ON THE OTHER HAND
*(James Birkhold, Bradenton, FL)*

**THE COURT** So, there are two DUIs [driving under the influence]. Sir, I very frankly am in sympathy with you in that you say you have problems. And you turned to alcohol for an escape, which of course is no answer, usually. It's more problem on top of problem. I can fully sympathize with you.

However, I can't believe that people that came home from the Vietnam War are any different than when they came home from any other war. Unfortunately, I don't sympathize with that position. People in the Vietnam War got all kinds of treatments like going to Canada and everything else that other people didn't get. I think they got no treatment any different from people that served in World War II for four years that didn't get a choice to go to Canada. I think that it's something that the people decided, it's a cop-out and I'll use it, very frankly, is how I feel about it. I'm not a doctor, but that's my position and you're asking me to act as a doctor and I'm not a doctor. I'm not going to say that you don't have problems. I'm sure you do if you feel you do.

On the other hand, I think you're a menace to society.

## THE PRESUMPTION
## OF INNOCENCE
*(Roger J. Dodd, Valdosta, GA)*

**COUNSEL**    I'm perfecting the record because it is my position that the Court incorrectly instructed the jury.

**THE COURT**    You show me authority to that effect.

**COUNSEL**    That presumption means that the defendant is, in fact, innocent as he sits there.

**THE COURT**    That's an impossibility for anyone to believe that, if he was innocent, he was sitting there. There would be no need for a trial.

## THE LOVE JUDGE
*(Stan Perlo, Los Angeles)*

**THE COURT**    First of all, let me ask you, did you want to file a motion to challenge me?

**DEFENDANT**    I might as well keep you. Might get someone worser.

**THE COURT**    You know, that's a possibility. I understand there are a couple of people in this building worse than me.

**DEFENDANT**    They call you the love judge.

**THE COURT**    I beg your pardon? What did they do, tell you I married someone the other day?

| | |
|---|---|
| DEFENDANT | They told me you are the love judge. Everybody come through here get love from you. |
| THE COURT | Somebody is trying to flimflam you. I don't know. They don't always leave happy. I try to be fair, and some people might not think my idea of fair is fair. I don't know. Anyway, at least for right now you are going to keep me, right? |
| DEFENDANT | I am going to keep you all the way. If I get dumped, I might as well get dumped by a pretty face. |
| THE COURT | Somebody gave him some clues. |
| COUNSEL | I got a feeling this guy is going to be an excellent pro per. |

## NO LOW IQ JURY
*(Jim Thompson, Sacramento)*

| | |
|---|---|
| COUNSEL | I would rest on my argument at this time. |
| THE COURT | Mr. Prosecutor. |
| DA | I can remember the days when trials were a search for the truth. |
| THE COURT | Well, yes, but we are dealing with the law as the Supreme Court has given it to us in this state. |
| DA | I understand that. |
| THE COURT | That's what I have to deal with. |
| DA | For the Court's information, in my |

argument, I would ask the Court to make the observation that the officer is between 5'9" and 5'10" and weighs approximately 180 pounds. I just want to get his size into the record.

COUNSEL    I have no objection to that and also that he carries a six-shot revolver.

THE COURT    Come on, gentlemen. You are not dealing with a retarded jury here. You're dealing with the Court.


## BRING IN THE JURY
*(Andrew Rubin, Santa Monica)*

THE COURT    Well, I'm going to point out that the significance of that is up to them. Let me give it a try. If I foul it up, it won't be the worse foul-up in this case. Bring them in.

COUNSEL    Sorry, but I gather that you will communicate to them that not all facts are necessarily relevant?

THE COURT    Well, I will probably say something like that. I don't know what I am going to say until I say it, but I'm going to try and convey to them that I am going to get a verdict out of them within the next forty-five minutes or kill myself right here in the courthouse before the end of the day. And if they get that message, we'll see how much they care.

# INSTRUCTIONS
*(Delgado Smith, Texarkana, TX)*

**THE COURT**   I will state for the record as I stated before, when these cases go on appeal for jury instructions, underline my words of wisdom, every time I get a case, it never fails. The defense always brings in their instructions at the conclusion of the case, and I am stumped with about 5,000 instructions I have never seen before.

If the appellate courts think I am going to go home and work on these things diligently in the evening, my answer to that is hogwash. I don't look at these stupid instructions anyway, so when they go on appeal, I wonder why they are given no thought by the trial judge, because the defense wants to keep me in the dark until the end.

This happens with all attorneys. It's a matter of style. Hoping the instructions will get screwed up on appeal. If they do, I don't give a good goddamn.


# SMART REMARK
*(Kenneth E. Houp, Jr, Austin)*

**THE COURT**   I understand your argument and I find it very intriguing, and I still don't know

any statutory authority for an ABC
officer to make a traffic stop. I'm not
saying the statute doesn't exist, I'm
saying that nobody has yet pointed that
out to me. But I think that it is a
fascinating question, but I think some
mind more intelligent than mine should
decide that.

COUNSEL    Well—

THE COURT    Let me rephrase that last comment.

COUNSEL    It cries out for a response, but I don't
think I'm going to say anything.

THE COURT    And I know your response would have
been, "You're not the dunce you seem to
be."

## JUDICIAL PERSUASION
*(Barry K. Newman, Dixon, CA)*

WITNESS    I wish to have a lawyer.

THE COURT    Why?

WITNESS    Why?

THE COURT    Yes.

WITNESS    Obvious reasons, I can't testify.

THE COURT    Why? Why?

WITNESS    Because I just don't need a fink jacket.

THE COURT    That doesn't grant you a right to a
lawyer. You answer the question or I will
put you away so long they will pipe air
into you.

Q. What did you do, after you went into your motel room and discovered these items had been taken?

A. I don't remember.

Q. Do you remember whether or not you came in contact with a couple of police officers later on?

A. I remember something of it.

THE COURT  You'd better start remembering.

WITNESS  I was under the influence of alcohol.

THE COURT  I don't care what you say you were. You'd better start remembering, and you'd better start telling the truth. Or we can make sure they know in the jail what you are doing [finking]. We can broadcast it over the P.A. system, so I would start telling the truth, and I would start remembering.

## NO SMILES ALLOWED
*(Delgado Smith, Texarkana, TX)*

THE COURT  It shall not happen again. We are not going to have defense lawyers arguing. I am glad you think it is funny, Mr. R.

MR. R.  Why do you think I think it is funny, Your Honor?

THE COURT  Because it is improper for you to smile and laugh—

MR. R.  I am not laughing, Your Honor.

THE COURT     —whenever I admonish a lawyer about improper conduct.

MR. R.     I am not smiling and laughing. I don't know what Your Honor is talking about.

THE COURT     You just did it.

MR. R.     If I have a pleasant expression on my face—

THE COURT     Every time I say it, you say it didn't happen. Are you saying you didn't smile to Mr. L. in front of all these people in the courtroom?

MR. R.     I said I had a pleasant expression, a smile on my face.

THE COURT     You admitted you had a smile on your face.

MR. R.     I don't know why you keep doing this to me. It had nothing to do with what Your Honor said.

THE COURT     If it didn't, you wouldn't have done it.

MR. R.     You don't know what I was talking to Mr. L. about; isn't that correct, Your Honor?

THE COURT     We all know exactly what is going on here, Mr. R. We know exactly what is going on. So when you smile as you are, agreeing with me, we all know what is going on.

## ALL NIGHT LONG
*(Jim Thompson, Sacramento)*

DA      Your Honor, it is now my intent to call Mr. Jones to testify. He was not excused by the Court. I don't know that he is around.

THE COURT      Mr. Bailiff, will you go out—you mean we are out of bailiffs? I have got to have somebody announce that Mr. Jones is wanted in this courtroom.

DETECTIVE      He is not in the hallway.

COUNSEL      It is almost unbelievable to me that any witness that we have not excused—This is the first witness in the whole case that someone has indicated should show up in two minutes.

THE COURT      He was told to remain in the courthouse, wasn't he, yesterday?

COUNSEL      I don't know what words the Court used, but I certainly didn't get the impression that he was supposed to go out in the hallway and paste himself to one of those seats and stay there.

THE COURT      Get me yesterday's transcript. (Pause) On page 636, I said, "All right, Mr. Jones, you are not to leave this courthouse." Isn't that right?

COUNSEL      You expected him to be out there last night?

THE COURT      All night, yes. All right, Counsel. You

want to give me any more objections
you have to putting Mr. Jones's statement into evidence, the preliminary
transcript?

# 6

# THE JURORS

*"The hungry judges soon the sentence sign,
And wretches hang that jurymen may dine."*
*ALEXANDER POPE*

*"It was a jury of average ignorance perfectly capable of determining
which side had the best attorney."*

*OLD JUDGES' AXIOM*

"Your honor, my client requests a change of venue."

# LET SLEEPING JURORS LIE

Former Detroit Tiger pitching great Denny McLain got into a heap of trouble several years ago. He went on trial, was convicted, and appealed. In *U.S. v. McLain*, 833 F.2d 1457 (11th Cir. 1987), the Court held McLain did not receive a fair trial due to the trial court's insistence on getting the trial over within too short a time period. To accomplish her goal, the judge started trial at 7:30 in the morning and went to 5:00 P.M. After a while, this took its toll on the jurors, who became inattentive and sleepy. In response, the judge ordered the bailiffs to pass food and coffee to them while they were seated in the jury box. They were also allowed to stand and stretch in the box while witnesses testified.

One juror expressed the sentiments of all when he requested that the judge open the curtains so that the jury could view the annual Tampa Gasparilla Parade go by while the trial was in process.

Sleeping jurors became quite a problem. The trial court observed that one juror had a "considerable problem in remaining with her eyes open." Defense Counsel responded that the juror did not respond when a recess was called or hear the call for coffee. "When the rest rose today to go out, she was still sitting down until someone moved her chair and woke her."

To all of this, the prosecutor disagreed that there was any harm with this juror remaining on the jury; he offered the following explanation: "She snapped up pretty quickly. I don't think anybody touched her. She could be subconsciously hearing."

## JURY POLL
### (Dale Cobb, Charleston, SC)

THE COURT   "If that be your verdict, so say you all."
TWO JURORS  "You all."

## JURY NOTE
### (Robert N. Harris, Los Angeles)

Please clarify instruction #7. If you are not feeling comfortable with the testaments of some officers but cannot provide any other rational conclusion, is your vote considered guilty by default?

## JUROR NOTE TO JUDGE:
## THE CURSE
### *(Mark Kaiserman, Santa Monica)*

On August 21st or 22 Juror #9 announced that she was going to put a voodoo curse on myself and another juror. I don't believe he heard this because of being involved in another conversation. The woman's posture and demeanor convinced me that she was serious. Although I am Christian and don't believe in voodoo, I do believe that to her it's real and constitutes a threat. [signed] Juror #8

P.S. I will advise you if further developments occur. I prefer not to bring the issue to light at this time. Prior to this, we have had a good relationship.

## JURY NOTE: MID-TRIAL
### *(James Wessel, Carson City)*

We, the jury, in the interest of an expeditious trial, and for the general reduction of immaterial and repetitious questioning; Do hereby recommend that a shocking collar device be securely fastened to plaintiff's counsel. The control of said device shall be entrusted to a responsible member of the jury panel to be selected following the next recess. We thank you for your support.

## JURY NOTE: POT CASE
*(Julianna Humphrey, San Diego)*

QUESTION 1    Can you send in one package of marijuana?

QUESTION 2    Can we smoke in the adjoining room so as not to bother nonsmokers?

## VOIR DIRE
*(Quin Denvir, Sacramento)*

Q.    Do you remember the context in which your husband brought the issue up?

PROSPECTIVE JUROR    Not really. I try not to listen when he talks.

## JURY DELIBERATES:
## VERDICT, A TOSS UP
*(Timothy A. Smith, Cincinnati)*

*The jury entered the courtroom at 1:45 P.M.*

THE COURT    Ladies and gentlemen, three things before we get back to the witness. The first thing is that I've been advised that there have been some people, not mentioning names or anything of that nature, who have been pitching coins in the hall. That happens to be against the law. It's gambling, and subject to prosecution. If it's going on, I suggest you cease it.

## VOIR DIRE
### (John Radin, Idaho Falls)

ROSPECTIVE JUROR  I'll voice an opinion. I think they ought to have public stonings. You know, have a big pit with bleachers, charge 50 cents a rock, and give the money to the school systems, you know, be a good deterrent.

## VOIR DIRE
### (Patsy Morris, Atlanta, GA)

COUNSEL  Okay. Now, is your feeling then that you have—is it so fixed that your opinion could not be changed by the evidence or the charge of the Court upon the trial of this case?

JUROR  May I say something?

COUNSEL  Yes, ma'am.

JUROR  The questions you're asking are not fitting my answers.

# JUROR QUESTIONNAIRE
*(Wendy Alderson, San Francisco)*

QUESTION    Please name the degrees, if any, you have, and all schools and colleges you attended, and your major areas of study.

ANSWER ON FORM    Electrical shock (used for cows) = damage brain. Cannot remember much some words. Should not affect my abilities as a juror.

# IF HE'S INNOCENT,
# I WON'T WORRY ABOUT HER FINGERS
*(Joel Hirschhorn, Miami)*

COUNSEL    Was there anything about this experience which would make it difficult for you to be fair in this case?

JUROR    I had a friend who was smoking a joint, and it was laced with PCP, and she chewed off two of her fingers.

COUNSEL    As a result of that, that is the kind of terrible experience we're talking about, would you find it difficult to be fair in this case?

JUROR    Not if the defense can prove he's innocent, no.

## VOIR DIRE
*(Earle Partington, Honolulu)*

Q.  Well, I mean, if a policeman gets up on the stand and says the defendant broke the law, is that all there is to it?

A.  Under oath. I believe him if he's under oath.

Q.  You would believe a policeman if he's under oath?

A.  That's right.

Q.  Just because he's a policeman?

A.  Regardless who. Everybody under oath.

Q.  So, it doesn't matter what they say, you'd believe 'em?

A.  I believe because they're under oath. Otherwise they'd be tried for perjury.

Q.  If a policeman testifies that the defendant drove his Volkswagen Beetle at 200 miles an hour down Kalakaua Avenue, would you believe that?

A.  Under oath I would.

Q.  If the policeman said the defendant had two heads the night that he arrested him, under oath, would you believe that?

A.  That's right.

COUNSEL  Move to disqualify.

THE JUROR  Under oath.

"After due deliberation, Your Honor, we the jury find ourselves in full agreement with the media, which has already tried and convicted the defendant."

# I CAN BE FAIR
*(Joan Markoff, Sacramento)*

THE COURT    All right. We're in the jury deliberation room with the juror. The defendant and both counsel are present. Can you tell us some of your concerns about being fair and objective?

A.    I look at it this way, the gentleman has thirteen counts against him. If he's here, he's guilty.

Q.    He's convicted? Why do we bring a jury in?

A.    That's the law. The man is entitled to a fair and impartial jury.

Q.    You mean, in your opinion he's guilty before he even starts the trial just because thirteen charges or counts have been filed?

A.    Yes.

Q.    Okay. We certainly don't criticize you for your candor, your honesty. Is there any reason that you can think of that might affect your ability to be fair and impartial?

A.    No.

## VOIR DIRE
*(Michael Arkelian, Sacramento)*

Q.  Could you imagine any case in which
you could personally vote for a death
penalty, or do you think you'd select life
without parole instead of death on every
occasion?

A.  Life in prison.

Q.  What you're telling me, and I'm not
trying to put words in your mouth, I just
want to make sure I understand what
you're saying. Is it correct that you're
telling me you can't imagine any case, no
matter how bad it is, how aggravated,
I've used a ridiculous example here in
the first couple of weeks with a couple of
people, let's say some guy, with no
excuse in the world, just a mean guy,
blew up an airplane with 400 people on
it and on that airplane was Mother
Teresa and Mrs. Aquino and 298 tiny
children, he killed them all in cold blood,
and you were on that jury. Are you
saying you still wouldn't vote for the
death penalty even in that case, is that
what you're telling me?

A.  I would think about it then.

Q.  Just a mean SOB. You can't imagine one
much meaner. But would you still feel
that it's not your place or the jury's

place, society's place to have a death penalty, even in such a case?

A. I don't have an answer. I'm not sure.

Q. Pretty tough one, isn't it?

A. Yes.

Q. I'm wondering if I can think of an even more extreme example.

COUNSEL Bishop Tutu, Your Honor.

THE COURT What?

COUNSEL Desmond Tutu.

THE COURT Okay. There you go.

Q. (by the Court) In addition to Mother Teresa, she's from India, someone suggested—you know who Bishop Tutu is in South Africa?

A. Yes.

Q. Probably a hero to most of the folks of your race these days, wouldn't you say? Suppose he was on that plane, this guy blew him up, could you vote for the death penalty then?

A. I don't know.

## OFF TO THE RACES
*(George Eskin, Ventura, CA)*

DA What do you think about psychologists? We have one right here on the panel. You are free to speak up.

JUROR　Don't you know I am free to speak up. I will tell you all there is nothing there. I could not care one way or the other. The only thing I want is Wednesday, Thursday, Friday, Saturday, and Sunday for the horse races. I don't want to be bothered. Present your case if you have no reasonable doubt, but if you have some kind of doubt—you better get me out of here if you got any doubt. If there is a slight bit of doubt, I am not going to convict somebody on a slight bit of doubt, but I will take the truth as best I can.

DA　Are you telling me I have to prove my case a hundred percent, beyond any doubt at all, with you?

JUROR　You just come out with the ninety-nine, ninety-four but you don't have to come up with the hundred percent. Would you prefer me to go and convict someone with some doubt? Could you sleep the night before if we convict a man with something?

THE COURT　I really think what she is getting at—

JUROR　Let her get at it and see what she tells me.

# PROFESSIONAL ENTERTAINER
## (Michael Tarlton, Placerville, CA)

PROSPECTIVE JUROR   Yes, sir. I'm a retired entertainer, and my husband is retired from the Air Force who now works for the Air Force as a civilian as an engineering technician supervisor.

THE COURT   I've got to ask. What field of entertainment were you in?

PROSPECTIVE JUROR   Do I have to answer that?

THE COURT   Well—

PROSPECTIVE JUROR   I'm a singer. I'm a vocalist.

THE COURT   Okay. I guess I shouldn't have asked. You had me nervous for a moment.

PROSPECTIVE JUROR   That maybe I might have remembered you or something? (Laughter) I didn't mean that part. Wait a minute. I didn't mean it like that. You have a naughty mind.


# INSIDER KNOWLEDGE
## (Roberta K. Thyfault, San Diego)

THE COURT   I have a note from the foreman, who says you need to talk to me.

JUROR   Yes, sir. I probably should have said this earlier, but in my mind I thought I could have discounted completely one witness's testimony if in my mind everything seemed to be logical, and I could come to a complete and total decision in my mind as to the guilt or innocence of the defendant. But as it stands right now, I know one of the witnesses, and I don't—and it's confused me completely. This is crazy.

THE COURT   How do you mean, you know one of the witnesses? One of the people who actually testified here?

JUROR   Yes, I know a girl that used to work with the witness, and I—you will think I'm nuts. She's [the witness] not female. She's a male.

THE COURT   Okay. I think I'm going to want to talk with these lawyers a little bit as to what—let me ask you the sixty-four-dollar question: Does this prevent you from being a fair and impartial juror?

JUROR   Well, if I was a professional juror, maybe it would be easier for me to make a decision. But under the circumstances—

THE COURT   I'll tell you, even if you were a professional juror, you would not have encountered this one.

# JUROR DISCHARGE
*(Marvin Schultz, Fresno)*

THE COURT   So I've entered a judgment of acquittal as to the charge against the defendant. It means your services are no longer required. So the good news is that you're discharged from further service in this case. The other good news is that you are to return Tuesday, January 12, at ten o'clock for another case.

JUROR #7   Come on, give us a break. This guy [the defendant] walks out of here scot free and we've got to come back.

# HAND SIGNAL
*(Mark J. Sullivan, Palm Springs)*

DA   Have you ever been cut off by an erratic driver?

JUROR   Of course.

DA   Do you ever retaliate against him?

JUROR   Never.

DA   Do you believe that it is ever appropriate to retaliate against an erratic driver?

JUROR   Certainly not.

DA   What is your normal response if you are cut off?

JUROR   I usually just give the guy the finger and drive off. What is your normal response if you are cut off?

## HARMLESS FOUL
*(David Carlton, Los Angeles)*

THE COURT   Any member of your immediate family or yourself ever been the victim of a crime or robbery?

JUROR   My mother had her purse snatched.

THE COURT   How long ago was that?

JUROR   Ten, fifteen years ago.

THE COURT   Was she hurt at all in the snatch?


## ADVENTURES OF THE UNHAPPY SUNSET JUROR
*(Carol A. Watson, Los Angeles)*

THE COURT   Good afternoon. Please answer the questions about yourself.

JUROR   I am divorced and have three children, aged twenty-eight, twenty-six, and eighteen. The older one is an exercise rider for the race track. The next one is a locksmith, and the eighteen-year-old is starting school. I had seven years active service in World War II and Korea. I had three prior jury experiences.

The first one was an assault and battery case and I asked the question, "What is battery?" and was immediately excused. The second case was a rape case which was dismissed right in the middle of trial based on the testimony of the victim. Then there was a burglary case and I was the jury foreman and it was a hung jury.

THE COURT  Are you retired?

JUROR  I got laid off so I am retired.

THE COURT  Retired involuntarily?

JUROR  Yes.

THE COURT  Have you ever been a victim of a crime?

JUROR  Two times. When I was eighteen, our house was robbed and they cleaned it out. They opened the door and carried everything off with a moving van.

THE COURT  Did anything ever come of it as far as a court case?

JUROR  No. Very unhappy. Just reported, and that was the last we heard. The next one was when I got hit over the head with a gallon bottle of liquid.

THE COURT  Do you want to tell us about that?

JUROR  I was down on Sunset Boulevard and I met this gal and her boyfriend, and we were kind of talking and they wanted a ride down the street and I said, "Why not?" I turned my back and *POW!*

THE COURT  Did they take property from you or money or your rings?

JUROR  It didn't knock me out and she was swinging a second time. I grabbed the bottle from her and set it down, trying to figure out what happened, because I was bleeding profusely, and she picked the bottle up again and tried to hit me again, and then I got the drift.

THE COURT    It doesn't take a house to fall on you. So what happened? Did you take it from her again?

JUROR    I took the bottle away from her again and I was going to hit her with it and then they split. I never reported it to the police.

THE COURT    Do you think the police officer might think you were—

JUROR    Whatever.

THE COURT    Okay, other than what you have already described, have you been a witness to a crime?

JUROR    Two times. Somebody hit a police officer on a motorcycle with an automobile and he literally slid right in front of my feet. I grabbed his radio for help and they responded. It was hit and run. That was the first crime. The second crime, I was on Sunset Boulevard again.

THE COURT    Did you live out that way? You don't have to answer that.

JUROR    No, I got divorced twelve years ago. That is my second home. There was this girl walking down the street and she walked by a driveway and a guy came from nowhere and grabbed her and started running with her. She was kicking and screaming and hollering, arms and legs going. I pulled the car around, and as soon as the headlights hit the scene he dropped her and her feet kept going, and she went that way and he went that way.

THE COURT  You were successful in thwarting the crime in progress?

JUROR  I hope.

THE COURT  Have you been accused of any crime?

JUROR  Three times. I was married to a woman who liked to beat on me. That was great, except it gets tiresome. We used to call the sheriff and she would calm down. On one occasion, I instructed her how to make a citizen's arrest. I got arrested and I went to jail, and the purpose was when we went to court I can tell my story. It didn't work out that way.

THE COURT  She was beating on you, but you told her how to make an arrest on you?

JUROR  Yes, she said I hit her, too, and I did. I slapped her.

THE COURT  What were you charged with?

JUROR  Assault and battery.

THE COURT  What happened?

JUROR  I had a trial and they never asked me any details. The judge said, "Did you slap her?" and I said, "Sure." Guilty. That cost $276.

THE COURT  Were you satisfied with the result?

JUROR  Totally unhappy. I thought she would be embarrassed and would never do it again.

THE COURT   It didn't work out that way?

JUROR   No.

THE COURT   What about the next time?

JUROR   The next time, after I got divorced, I met a woman in Redondo Beach. She rented a room and we got involved and she accused me of forcing myself upon her.

THE COURT   What were you charged with?

JUROR   Well, it ended up with disturbing the peace. They plea-bargained.

THE COURT   Were you satisfied with the result?

JUROR   No.

THE COURT   Because?

JUROR   The way the lawyer handled it.

THE COURT   The lawyer for which side?

JUROR   My side. You learn as these things go.

THE COURT   Was it a public defender?

JUROR   No. I gave him hard cash.

THE COURT   Okay. That always hurts. So the only difficulty in that case was the lawyer, then?

JUROR   Yeah, and his advice that I paid for.

THE COURT   Okay. Now the third crime.

JUROR   The third and last time was prostitution.

THE COURT   You were charged with prostitution?

JUROR   Well, I guess, but the pretty girl was a police officer.

THE COURT   When did that take place?

JUROR   About three years ago.

THE COURT   Where? Let me guess. Somewhere on the Sunset Strip. Was it on the Sunset Strip?

| | |
|---|---|
| JUROR | Yes. |
| THE COURT | Did you have a trial? |
| JUROR | A tremendous trial. A jury trial. |
| THE COURT | Did it come out to your satisfaction? |
| JUROR | No. Like all guilty people, I was innocent and police officers do lie. |
| THE COURT | Well, now, you told us about a number of things that happened to you with the court system, most of which you are unhappy with. |
| JUROR | Oh, yes. |
| THE COURT | Can you state with unequivocal certainty that you could be fair and impartial to both sides? |
| JUROR | Definitely. |

## COOL UNDER FIRE
*(Terry Mackey, Cheyenne, WY)*

| | |
|---|---|
| THE COURT | Please be seated. Court's in session. Defendant's here, Counsel and the jury. Mr. Juror, I understand there's a problem out near your house? |
| JUROR | Yes. |
| THE COURT | I understand the problem is that there's a fire down there and they say they might have to evacuate your wife? |
| JUROR | Yeah, they might. |
| THE COURT | How do you feel about that? |
| JUROR | Need some rain. |

## VOIR DIRE
*(Marvin O. Teague, Austin)*

Q. How long have you had that opinion about the death penalty?

A. Since I noticed a lot of people doing a little more crime. I feel, my own opinion, that you go back to the olden days and put a cross down and nail 'em to it and then do what you feel. This is my opinion of that.


## NOW I HEAR YOU
*(James Joseph Lynch, Sacramento)*

THE COURT   Mr. S., what is your occupation?

JUROR   What's that?

THE COURT   (Shouting) What is your occupation?

JUROR   Oh, I am retired, sir.

THE COURT   Mr. S., do you have a hearing problem?

JUROR   What's that?

THE COURT   (Shouting) Do you have a hearing problem?

JUROR   Oh, well ever since I have had a stroke, I have not been able to hear so well out of my good ear.

THE COURT   Counsel?

COUNSEL   Capacity, Your Honor.

THE COURT   Mr. S., you are excused.

JUROR   What's that?

THE COURT   (Shouting) You are excused.

## A JUROR'S PERSPECTIVE
*(Ken Wells, Sacramento)*

JUROR    That this system works at all is just
         amazing. Because you people are not
         unlike children who've bagged a moose
         with a slingshot and dragged the big
         carcass home and drop it off outside the
         kitchen door, fully expecting the adults
         inside to take care of it, in much the
         same regard, sir, the two of you are
         going to push your evidence up here to
         the jury box and expect us to do the
         same with it.

# 7

# MALAPROPS

*"When ideas fail, words come in very handy."*

GOETHE

*"The majority of all laws are nothing but privileges, that is, a tribute paid by all to the convenience of some few."*

BECCARIA

*"Your Honor, my client is ready to sing."*

## WELL THOUGHT OF★
### (Paul R. Huscher, Des Moines)

Counsel    Mr. Penis, I'm handing you what the witness has wrote.

DA    May the record reflect that my name is Powers?

Counsel    I'm sorry. What am I calling you?

DA    You called me Mr. Penis.

Counsel    I'm sorry, Mr. Powers. I'm sorry.

DA    Currently, I have quite a reputation in the prosecutor's office; however, I did not know that you join in it.


## SLIP OF THE TONGUE
### (David Call, San Bernadino)

Mr. B.    I object to that.

Mrs. T.    This is my argument.

Mr. B.    I have to object to this. This is a

misstatement of the law. I won't
interrupt any more other than to ask for
an opportunity to tell you what I believe
is correct.

Mrs. T.   Your Honor, I sat on my tongue until
it's three inches longer during Mr. B.'s
argument; and I am going to sit on his
tongue in a minute, if the Court will
allow me to do so. Well, no, I retract
that statement. Strike that.

Mr. B.   I hope no one provides a transcript of
that to my wife.


## PLAIN SPEAKING
*(Anonymous Bosch, Paris, ID)*

A.   Will you ask that question again, sir?
Q.   Sure. Most judges talk like lawyers
because they were a lawyer at one time,
and it tends to confuse things. It could
be said simpler if I can remember how I
used to do it before I became a lawyer.


## A ROSE BY ANY OTHER NAME
*(John Lee, City of Industry, CA)*

THE COURT   There is one question that I have about
your points and authorities, though. Just

referring to page 17, line 3, you indicated no similar provision bars the persecutor from calling any of his witnesses. Did you really mean to call him persecutor?

Counsel   Depends on one's perspective, Your Honor.

## QUEEN'S ENGLISH
### *(Constance Crooker, Portland, OR)*

A.   First I had asked him where he was headed, and he said he was going to Los Angeles, California.

Q.   And do you recall if that was in English or Spanish?

A.   That was in English. I'm certain he said he was going to Los Angeles.

Q.   I'm sorry, so your question to him was in English and what language was his answer in?

A.   Well, he said, "Los Angeles," so it was in English.

## CUTTING REMARK
### *(Leslie Abramson, Los Angeles)*

DA   Your Honor, he is on a statement, he is on the witness list, he has been called.

We know where he is. I'm intending to call him. I don't know why I'm being circumcised.

COUNSEL   Because you are Jewish, but beyond that—circumscribed, Alex.

DA   That too.

## SLIP OF TONGUE II
*(David Berman, San Diego)*

PROSECUTOR   We have other witnesses, yes, Your Honor. In particular, one counsel had asked that I have present the other agent who was in the vehicle that made the vehicle stop. I think that agent's testimony would be duplicitous.

## AWARD
*(Louis R. Miles, Salem, OR)*

Q.   Have you ever received any honors or prizes for your work in the area of child sexual abuse?

A.   Yes. I was given an award for my contribution to sexual abuse in the state of Idaho last year.

## DA FINAL ARGUMENT★
### *(W. Mark McKnight, Portland, OR)*

DA   The defense attorney had hardly anything to cross-examine him on. You can ask any questions about the sodomy that he wants to ask. He could have asked him, "Now, tell me in detail what did his penis look like?" Could have asked him for that, but he didn't because that's pretty hard.

## BUTCHERED WORDS
### *(Richard Krech, Oakland)*

Mr. W.   Objection. That mesmerizes his testimony.

The Court   Overruled.

Mr. W.   Your Honor, I object; relevance in view of the earlier rulings.

The Court   Mr. S.?

Mr. S.   This goes to her credit and voracity.

## VOIR DIRE
### *(H. Dean Steward, Santa Ana)*

Prospective Juror   I live in LA. I'm a seamstress, unemployed. I'm married, and my husband is an assembler of penal wear.

## DIRECTIONS TO DELIVERY SERVICE
### (Paul Caruso, Beverly Hills)

INSTRUCTIONS   Please file directly in Dept. 47, conform copy and have the Judge executed. Thank you.

## JURY VIEW
### (K. Ronald Bailey, Huron, OH)

DA   All right, Mr. C., is it not a fact that this witness came into this Court here and admitted having sexual relations with you in open court, in front of the jury?

## FATE WORSE THAN DEATH
### (Frank Nageotte, San Diego)

COUNSEL   Under our law there is absolutely no crime for which the death penalty is automatic. What that means is that that penalty is a possible penalty in those cases where murder in the first degree with special circumstances is found. And, again, if that occurs, then, it is the jury—not the judge, the jury—that makes the decision as between wife without the possibility of parole or death.

## HARDSHIP EXCUSAL
*(Stanley Simrin, Bakersfield, CA)*

THE COURT   Mr. Juror, I've talked to the lawyers about your problem and I understand your funeral has already started, so I will excuse you from this case and you may go to the funeral and then go back to work.

## COURT ORDER II
*(Gary Nelson, San Diego)*

THE COURT   Defendant is present with Counsel. Deputy District Attorney present. Counsel stipulates to the case being fabricated on Counts I, II, III, and IV until the end of the jury trial.

## SQUIRT GUN CHARGE
*(Dale Cobb, Charleston, SC)*

*Charge returned by Grand Jury:*
   Indictment for Illegal Pissession of a Pistol. True Bill.

## HORRIBLE TYPO
*(Jill Schlictmann, San Francisco)*

Your affiant has spoken with the informant and has determined that he has knowledge/understanding of the identification of the narcotic cocaine and its trafficking. On 04/22/89, officers from Narcotics Enforcement Team arrived armed with a search warrant signed by the Horrible Judge for the suspect's residence. Upon searching the house, records were found/seized.

## SLIP OF THE TONGUE
*(Barry Newman, Santa Ana)*

Q. Is the report that you wrote in regards to this incident complete and accurate?

A. Yes, ma'am.

Q. Is it a fair statement that all the elements in this report are important?

DA Objection, Your Honor, it's irrelevant what's fair in this case.

## WHERE AGAIN?*
*(Herbert A. Bloom, San Mateo)*

Q. Where was your daughter when you and he had sexual intercourse?

DA Wait a second, Counsel. We haven't established that.

COUNSEL  I tried to.

DA  No, you didn't. Ask her if she had sexual intercourse with him. Not, "When did you have sexual intercourse?"

COUNSEL  I thought she indicated that she had a romantic relationship with the man.

DA  That's not the same as sexual intercourse.

COUNSEL  Did you ever have sexual intercourse with him in Mexico?

A.  Yes.

Q.  All right. Now, where?

A.  For goodness sakes. On the floor in the living room. Would you like more details?

## DEADLY WEAPON COMPLAINT*
### (Steve Rease, Monterey)

I [Officer P.], state upon information and belief, that the female defendant did in the County of Monterey, State of California, commit the crime of VIOLATION OF CALIFORNIA PENAL CODE SECTION 12020, a MISDE-MEANOR, committed as follows, to wit: That at said time and place the said defendant did willfully and un-lawfully manufacture, cause to be manufactured, im-port into the State of California, keep for sale, offer and expose for sale, and give, lend, and possess an in-strument and weapon of the kind commonly known as a dick.

## LETTER OF RECOMMENDATION
### (Louis Coffin, New Bedford, MA)

To Honorable Judge,

This is a letter concerning John D. and his incarceration. He has been in the Alcohol (AA) Annoyance Program, here at Southeastern Correctional Center, for the past four and a half months. And up until this very day he has been a very active member of the Foundation's Group (AA). I know if he was given another chance to attend Alcohol (AA) Annoyance's on the streets, he will be a Project to us here at Southeastern Correctional Center, to make us look at what he did.

## PROBATION REVOCATION
### (Andrew Rubin, Santa Monica)

THE COURT    You have to realize the standards are different at a probation revocation hearing versus a trial of the matter or even a sentencing.

DEFENDANT    Oh, different in what respect, Your Honor? I still have a right to a fair hearing.

THE COURT    Yes, you do.

DEFENDANT    I have a right to counter allegations. I have a right, you know, to those basic things there. And if you look at the probation report back here under "Analysis," okay, you know, it sounds like this was written on Joseph Mengele, or somebody.

THE COURT  Oh, I think you're being overly dramatic.

DEFENDANT  No, I ain't, no, no. He says the defendant has no redeeming social qualities. Well, that made me as a vegetable, you know. No redeeming social qualities. I have a psychologist's report here. He says, "Well, the defendant has a high prosperity for violence." It don't say that in this—

THE COURT  Prosperity for violence?

DEFENDANT  Yes, Your Honor. It says I have a high prosperity for drug abuse, too.


## MAN AT WORK
*(John Yzurdiaga, Los Angeles)*

Q.  What's your job, please?

A.  I'm a sales rep for Wonder Bread.

Q.  And what were you doing behind the Grocery Warehouse on October 12, 1987, at about seven o'clock in the morning?

A.  I was working my bread.

Q.  Working your bread?

A.  I was in the bowels of the back of the truck, working my bread.

## LEG IN MOUTH DISEASE

A Macomb County judge, citing what he believed to be a white man's rage over his wife's infidelity with a black man, convicted the man of manslaughter instead of murder Thursday in the ax-slaying of his wife.

Macomb County Circuit Judge . . . said from the bench Thursday, "Here's the defendant . . . for the first time, faced with the horribleness of an infidelity. Not only an infidelity—and I do not wish to be called a racist, but we are in a court of law and a spade has to be called a spade—but an infidelity with a black man."

*Detroit Free Press,* 1/28/84

## NOBODY IS STILL HERE
### *(David Ellenbogen, Washington, DC)*

THE COURT  Is everybody here? Nobody is here.

DA  Well, I take exception to that, Your Honor.

THE COURT  Well, I mean nobody who is anybody.

DA  I withdraw my objection.

## PROBATION RECOMMENDATION
### *(Donald Rehkopf, Jr., Rochester, NY)*

Recommendation: Probation with the following special conditions:

1. Community Service.
2. Restitution.
3. It is recommended that a Certificate of Relief from diabetes be deferred at this time.


## DEAF FENCE ATTORNEY
*(Bill Dawson, Birmingham, AL)*

DA    Defense Counsel is accountable to you [the jury].

Counsel    Judge, I object to that. I object to him referring to me as a cannibal, Judge.

The Court    He said accountable.

Counsel    A what?

The Court    He said accountable, not a cannibal.

Counsel    It sounded like cannibal to me and I object.


## MALAPROP
*(Earl Bute, New York City)*

Counsel    Would you believe, Your Honor, that was going to be my very next question?

The Court    Well, I thought I'd hurry it up.

Counsel    You're a very prescient judge.

The Court    Well, I've been present all afternoon.

## DOES HE OR DOESN'T HE?
*(Anonymous Bosch, Paris, ID)*

WITNESS     And I kind of made the remark
            something about as he was an older man,
            he would be curious as to which chick
            was his—or something of that.

THE COURT   Give me that again. Because he was an
            older man, what?

WITNESS     When, you know, as he got to be an
            older man, he would wonder which chick
            was his.

THE COURT   When he was an older man, he would
            wonder which, what?

WITNESS     Chick, as if the baby was going to be a
            girl, is what—

THE COURT   What is that word? I don't get it.
            "Chick?"

WITNESS     Chick.

COUNSEL     Chick—meaning, as I understand it,
            whether the baby was his.

THE COURT   Yeah, but tell me what that word is. Is
            it C-H-I-P or C-H-I-T? What is it?

WITNESS     I don't know. It is a phrase a lot of
            people use about a young girl, like "a
            chick."

THE COURT   You say "chick," C-H-I-C-K?

WITNESS     Yes.

THE COURT   Oh, I know what a chick is.

## MOUTHFUL
*(Vic Mature, Washington, DC)*

JUDGE  What made you bite the police officer?
WITNESS  He stuck his arm in my mouth.


## WIRED TIGHT
*(Michael Tarlton, Placerville, CA)*

Q.  You actually went inside her home that evening?
A.  Yes.
Q.  Were you wired that night?
A.  Yes, sir, I was. I should say I had a body wire on me.
THE COURT  We have encountered that question earlier. Wired can have another meaning.
COUNSEL  What other meaning does it have, Your Honor?
THE COURT  See me privately and I will straighten you out about that.

# 8

# THE POLICE

"It is far pleasanter to sit comfortably in the tree's shade rubbing red pepper into a poor devil's eyes than to go about in the hot sun hunting up evidence."

AXIOM OF THE CONSTABLES OF INDIA

"And put in every honest hand a whip
To lash the rascals naked through the world . . ."

WILLIAM SHAKESPEARE,  OTHELLO (IV, II, 142)

# TOO MUCH
*(Stephen McCue, Albuquerque)*

DA    What information were you given, if any, about whose residence this was?

OFFICER    At that time, we were informed that it was the residence of one of the individuals who had been arrested at a motel in reference to the transaction of narcotics.

DEFENDANT    (Speaks in Spanish).

DA    May I continue, Your Honor?

THE COURT    Well, I think we should have a translation of what the defendant said.

INTERPRETER    The statement, Your Honor, was: "I did not think that these people would lie so much."

THE COURT    You may continue.

## CALL 911
*(Danny Fabricant, Ventura, CA)*

THE COURT    And on the facts presented in this
trial—and not intending to be
patronizing of one side or the other or
unnecessarily glib—given the state of the
record at this point, if one of the jurors
was confronted with a dangerous situation
and had to put 20 cents in the phone to
call for help, the probability is they
would call the Hell's Angels as opposed
to the law enforcement officers that were
involved in this case.

## POLICE REPORT*
*(Delgado Smith, Texarkana, TX)*

The victim said that the defendant pulled his penis
two times and then the police came.

## POLICE VERSION OF TRUTH
*(Dan Factor, Redondo Beach, CA)*

Q.    Okay. Did he tell you that he located
Victim Four's vehicle on Catalina Street?
A.    Yes.
Q.    When did he do that?

A. Let's see. Approximately about fifteen minutes after I made my broadcast.

Q. Did he say that he saw two male Hispanics walking southbound on Catalina Street?

A. Not during our broadcast, no. That was after we were at the station and got the story together.

## ARRESTING LOGIC
### (Richard K. Renn, York, PA)

*Officer's explanation for arresting three young men for underage drinking:*

A. I told him I normally would not cite people for underage drinking in this instance if they wouldn't have acted in the manner that they did. I usually try to give people breaks in this type of instance because I know people drink underage, but when I stopped them, smelled that they were drinking, found three bottles open, two closed, there's three people, all they have to do as far as I'm concerned on the scene, which is common for me, not for everybody, just say, hey, I'm sorry, I was drinking, let us throw these away, but no, they immediately come at me, tell me, oh, God, we just came here a few seconds

ago, we don't have no idea how this got
here, that tells me that they deserve to
be written rather than give a break, so I
didn't give them a break.

Q. So if someone admits to violating the
law, you give them a break, and if
someone claims innocence, you write
them up?

A. Correct. Police discretion.

Q. So much for the presumption of
innocence.

## POLICE REPORT:
## DYING DECLARATION*
*(Gary Scherotter, Palm Springs)*

On my arrival, I found the victim on his back, face
up, and talking to two Mexican male subjects. I walked
up to the victim and saw some blood on his chest and
stomach area. I then removed my knife from my gun
belt and cut the victim's white T-shirt to expose his
injuries. Upon doing so, I saw what appeared to be
four puncture wounds on the right side of his chest.
It appeared to me that a projectile had entered his
chest at a 30-degree angle, which would have placed
the projectile going through the victim's heart. With
such injuries, and in my experience investigating numerous murders over the past eighteen years, there was
no question in my mind that the victim would be expir-
ing shortly. I then attempted to get a dying declaration
from the victim.

I advised him that he had been shot numerous times in the chest and that one of the projectiles had punctured his heart. I advised him he only had a short time to live and would he give me a dying declaration as to who had shot him. He replied, "Yes, I have a declaration to make." I asked him what that was. He lifted his right hand, made a fist, exposing his center finger, and stated, "Go fuck yourself," and I ended my interview with the victim.

## COP CAR
### (Bruce Schweiger, Los Angeles)

Q. Officer, you were traveling with a partner, is that correct?

A. Yes, sir.

Q. Was he driving, or were you driving?

A. I was driving.

Q. You indicated that you were driving what is referred to as an unmarked car. Are we talking about a late model American sedan with blackwall tires and no hubcaps?

A. No, sir.

Q. So it was not a plainly marked police car?

A. I don't know what you mean by "plainly marked." It had hubcaps. It was a 1986 Chevy Impala.

Q. Which means? I mean, is it the kind of

car that every hype and thief on the
street will spot as a police car a block
away?

DA      Objection. Calls for speculation.
THE COURT      Overruled. You may answer.
WITNESS      Does that include attorneys?

## FROM A POLICE REPORT
*(Fred Herro, Monterey)*

Contacted: Small informant, approximately two
years old.

## JUST CHECKING*
*(Michael Piccaretta, Tucson, AZ)*

PROSECUTOR      Officer, did the defendant make any
comment to you during the recess just a
few moments ago?

A.      Yes, he did.
Q.      What did he say?
A.      As he stepped out the door, he stood
facing me, and he said, "You lying
motherfucker."

PROSECUTOR      Your witness.
COUNSEL      Were you lying?

## ALONE RANGER
*(Susan Peninger, Bakersfield, CA)*

Q. Were you the lone ranger on duty that night?
A. I was a park ranger on duty that night.
Q. I mean the only one, the lone—
A. You mean alone?
Q. Alone.
A. Yes, I was.


## POLICE REPORT
*(William Bloss, New Haven, CT)*

The accused was observed parked on Downing Street at Peck Street in the middle of the intersection for several minutes talking and cleaning out his truck. His actions did make it difficult for the residents and narcotic buyers to pass: he was charged accordingly.


## LIFE IMITATES LIFE
*(Bruce Lyons, Fort Lauderdale)*

Q. Would you tell us your name, please?
A. My name is Sergeant S.
Q. You're the same sheriff who we deposed on July 28, 1988?
A. For all intents and purposes, yes.

Q. You haven't changed in . . .

A. I think I've grown and matured in certain ways, but I'm the same person, yes.

Q. For the record, would you indicate in what ways you've matured, and indicate the source of that maturity?

A. Well, I see life as a learning experience, and so I hope to learn on a daily basis. I feel like Dan Quayle in some of the questions that he was asked.

Q. Frankly, I know Dan Quayle, and you're nothing like him.

A. I think that remark was uncalled for, but I'm glad to hear that I'm not like Dan Quayle.

## I DON'T GOTTA SHOW YOU NO STINKING BADGES
*(Danny Fabricant, Ventura, CA)*

Q. Detective, why did you bring a photograph of your badge with you today instead of your badge?

A. Because the last time I testified, my actual badge, if I would have shown it up here on the stand, would have been admitted as evidence.

## DOWN IN HIS CUPS
*(Jon Schoenhorn, Hartford, CT)*

SHERIFF    I ask that Counsel—I don't want that water on his desk. Will you instruct him otherwise?

DEFENSE COUNSEL    Your Honor, I can see perhaps there is a problem with a glass, although I would disagree, or concede his concern, but I was given a paper cup. I don't understand the concern. I have a slight cold and I am going to need this during the afternoon.

SHERIFF    You got your cup, just put it up here on the clerk's desk.

THE COURT    Well, is there a policy now?

SHERIFF    Well, it's a security reason, Your Honor.

DEFENSE COUNSEL    Your Honor, it has to be an arbitrary reason. I have a paper cup with water in it. The only security concern I can imagine is perhaps if my client wishes to drown himself in the cup.

## I DO BE BILINGUAL
*(Andrew Rubin, Santa Monica)*

Q.   Do you speak Spanish, Officer?
A.   Yes, I do.
Q.   Are you fluent in Spanish?
A.   Yes, I do.

## FORENSIC GROPER⋆
### *(Paul Buckley, Milton, MA)*

A. There's no doubt in my mind there was something in his groin area.

Q. You never grabbed him by the crotch before that, had you?

Q. No.

Q. So you don't know how well endowed he was or not, do you?

A. Well, I don't know how well endowed he was, but I felt it had nothing to do with his endowments.

Q. And you're familiar with grabbing crotches?

A. Well, on occasions I've done it at the airport, sir.

## THE UNKNOWN ANSWER
### *(John C. McBride, Boston)*

Q. And in this particular case, it's fair to say that there was no concern for anybody's safety, at least in connection with the defendant being a danger to anybody?

A. I was not aware that he was indexed in the NADDIS computer prior to conducting that search.

Q. Apart from not being indexed in NADDIS, was there any concern expressed at the

*"This time, let me do the talking."*

briefing session that he or anybody in that residence would present a danger to the officers executing the warrant?

A. There was unknown knowledge at that time—

Q. I'm sorry?

A. There was unknown knowledge at that time—

Q. There was unknown knowledge?

A. Yes. There was no knowledge at that time that gave us intelligence that we would be going into an armed situation.

## COMING UNSTUCK
*(Robert O. Switzer, San Antonio)*

COUNSEL    I'll move on.

Q. During the struggle, first you had him around the neck, then Officer G. had him around the neck. When Officer G. had him around the neck, where were you?

A. I had gotten up off the floor again. The defendant had gotten back up off the floor. They were both standing up. G. had him around the neck. We continuously were shouting to him to spit out the packet.

The defendant told us later that it wasn't the fact that he didn't want to spit it out,

but it was stuck to the roof of his mouth.
And since he was not spitting it out, since
he was still struggling with us trying to break
free of our grip, I kicked the subject twice in
the groin area. The second kick the packet
came out, it went to the floor, and I
retrieved the packet.

Q. The technique of kicking someone in the
groin area, is that more karate or
something that you would learn in police
procedures?

A. For something like this, I couldn't even
tell you if it's either/or. I do know that
it causes a great expulsion of breath,
which it did in this case.

Q. And it worked?

A. Yes, it did.

Q. In that sense, it was a good police
procedure because it achieved the result
that you desired?

A. And it does not cause you any
permanent lasting damage.


## THE SKULKER
*(George Henry Newman, Philadelphia)*

Q. That's why you stopped him, because he
was walking along in a sulking manner?

A. Skulking. S-K-U-L-K-I-N-G.

Q. Can you demonstrate what that is,
Detective? What does that mean?

A. Can I demonstrate it for you?

Q. Yes. Skulking manner, what is that?

A. I can demonstrate it for you.

Q. Would you kindly do that?

A. I'm going to need a crowd of people, and I will show you exactly what he did.

Q. There's enough people. We have enough people. Show us.

WITNESS For the sake of argument, this would be a large crowd. Okay, we are going to simulate that this large crowd is in this area right here. Okay, there is a large crowd of people. The defendant, when I come up, was in this crowd of people backing out this way, coming out and looking to where the officers were, which is over the crowd, as he comes into the wall—there's people all back here—until he reached this area where the wall was. Now, he is coming down the wall, looking in that area coming down the wall this way, backing up, when I stopped him.

THE COURT Indicating bent over from the waist with one hand against the wall being drawn along the wall; is that right?

WITNESS Yes, coming away from the crowd, which would be east on York Street on the south side.

THE COURT I would say that's a pretty good demonstration of a skulking, one of the best skulkings I have seen.

## FIELD SOBRIETY TEST
*(Roger Falk, Wichita, KS)*

Q. Now the next test that you asked him to perform was to count backwards from 20 to 0. Is that correct?

A. Yes.

Q. Now once again, did you give him an example?

A. No, I didn't. I just asked him to count backwards from 20 to 0.

Q. Would you count backwards from 20 to 0.

A. 20, 19, 18, 17, 16, 15, 14, 13, 11, 10, 9, 8, 7, 6, 5, 4, 3, 2, 1.

Q. Officer, have you been drinking this evening?

A. No, I haven't.

Q. You realize that you missed a number in there?

A. I—yes.

Q. But that isn't any sign that you're under the influence of alcoholic beverages at this time, is it?

A. No.

Q. Because you haven't been drinking. Now then, Officer, the next test that you asked Mr. L. to perform was to walk heel to toe. Is that correct?

A. Yes, it is.

Q. Now in that particular test, I believe your testimony was that you instructed

him to take six steps forward, pivot, and
return five steps.

A. Right.

Q. Now, Officer, let's back up against the
rail there for just a second. Would you
take six steps forward for me, heel to
toe—

A. Yes.

Q. —and pivot and take five steps back?

A. Okay.

Q. Officer, just so the record is clear, you
had a little problem with the pivot there,
didn't you?

A. Yes, I did. I was expecting to pivot the
other way and I didn't.

A. Now, once again, you haven't been
drinking, have you?

A. No, I haven't.

A. Now, sir, my client also explained to you
that he had undergone surgery on his
knee, had he not?

A. Yes, he did.

Q. And that he had a pin and at least three
screws in his knee that were holding his
knee together. Is that correct?

A. Yes.

Q. There was another test that you asked
my client to perform on that evening,
wasn't there?

A. Yes, there was.

Q. That was the finger and the nose test?

A. Yes, there was.

Q. Would you please tell us what the correct procedure is?

A. On that evening I did ask him if he would extend his arms out, and with his left hand touch the tip of his nose three times, and then with his right hand would be the same procedure. Plus, I, at the time I was explaining to him, I was showing him how I wanted him to do it.

A. That's standing with your heels together, I believe?

A. Yes.

Q. Is that also done with your eyes closed?

A. Yes, and with the head tipped back.

Q. I'd like you to close your eyes.

A. Okay.

Q. I'd like you to extend your arms.

A. (Witness indicates).

Q. I'd like you to tilt your head back. Now then, Officer, I'd like you to touch the tip of your nose with your right index finger three times.

A. (Witness indicates).

A. Would you do that with your left hand also, sir?

A. (Witness indicates).

Q. So the record is clear, sir. Would it be a correct statement that on the first try with, I believe it was your right hand, you touched the bridge of your nose?

A.  Yes, I did.

Q.  Again, that's not any indication you're under the influence, is it, sir?

A.  That would be one step at it, yeah.

(Later)

THE COURT  This is one of those cases that you sort of hate to decide because of the technicality of the law, but yet it is necessary that we observe those technicalities because they are fundamental to all of our rights. I have always wondered a little bit why police officers went through somewhat of a charade of giving people field sobriety tests when without somehow or another knowing the person's—I think I could take all those tests and probably flunk them all because I'm not all that well coordinated an individual. Without knowing that about a person, I really wonder why they think that they really prove the person's sobriety or insobriety. It was rather graphically shown by the officer himself. Apparently, he and I are kind of the same. We're not real well coordinated.

## SEIZE THE FRUIT

In an arrest for urinating in public, "it is unlikely that an officer would attempt to seize either instrumentality used to commit the crime or the fruits thereof." So he just took defendant's wallet, a seizure that the trial court condemned.

*People v. Smith,* 34 Cal.3d 251 (1983)

## POLICE REPORT:
## A STUDY IN EUPHEMISM
*(Jason Cox, Hayward, CA)*

I then directed the suspect's head toward the pavement in order to eliminate his hand from getting under his body via this route because the suspect was resisting by holding his head up even after I attempted to direct it down with little force and I was required to use more force causing his head to impact the pavement.

## INSUFFICIENT IQ TO ARREST
*(Ezekiel Perlo, Encino, CA)*

COUNSEL   Officer, at this point in your own mind, did you consider him to be a suspect in the homicide?

OFFICER   No. I really did not have enough intelligence to make that decision.

## DEATH PENALTY CASE SECURITY
### (Mark Kaiserman, Los Angeles)

COUNSEL   Sheriff, what concerns would you point to specifically that would require increased security during that period of time?

SHERIFF   I did mention concern for the defendants themselves and they are here present.

Q.   You have concerns for the defendants themselves?

A.   I do.

Q.   That they might be killed?

A.   Yes.

Q.   Isn't that what you're seeking in this prosecution?

## STEALTH RADAR
### (Richard K. Renn, York, PA)

Q.   Now, you were sitting concealed from oncoming traffic, is that correct?

A.   If you were eastbound traffic, that's correct, you would not be able to see me.

Q.   And you were radar-shooting eastbound traffic?

A.   That's correct.

Q.   Why did you conceal yourself?

A.   If you run radar out in the open, people have a tendency to slow down before they see you.

Q. Do they now? Isn't that why you run radar, to make people slow down?

A. That's correct.

Q. So more people would slow down if they saw you than if they didn't see you.

A. That's speculating on my part. I couldn't answer that.

Q. Well, no, it's not speculating. You just answered the question.

A. Our job is to enforce the speed limit and, you know, if people are out there speeding, you know, and we're out in the open, how are you gonna, you know, enforce the speed limit?

Q. Well, it makes people go within the speed limit, doesn't it?

A. I don't see how this is relevant.


## POLICE REPORT
*(Anonymous Bosch, Paris, ID)*

The defendant was one of the three males that I saw. He was out of breath, had a bloody lip, and didn't speak very well English.

## POLICE REPORT*
*(Garrick Lew, Oakland, CA)*

After I told him that he was the suspect and he denied it, I told him, "The next time you run from a police officer, you are probably going to"—and I quote myself, "Get your fucking head blown off; don't ever do it again," at which time we stuffed him in the car.

## ANOTHER DUI FIELD TEST
*(Blackie Burak, Concord, MA)*

Q. Now, Officer, after the modified position of attention, what was the next field sobriety test you asked him to perform?

A. That was the finger dexterity test.

Q. And could you explain that to us, please?

A. Sure. I'll explain it to you just like I explain to anybody that I would contact on the street in this situation. All you do is start with your thumb touching your index finger, and you count out loud like this:

1, 2, 3, 4, and back the other way, 4, 2, 3, 1.

You do it three times in a row like this: 1, 2, 3, 4; 4, 3, 2, 1; 1, 2, 3, 4; 4, 2, 3, 1; 1, 2, 3, 4; 4, 3, 2, 1. Three times, all in a row.

THE COURT  Okay. Now, while he's got his right foot in the air, which leg is he standing on?

A.  His left leg.

Q.  Which leg was broken?

A.  The left leg.

Q.  So he's standing on his broken leg?

A.  With the brace, yes.

Q.  Okay. And you took that into consideration?

A.  Yes, I did.

Q.  And it's your testimony that that's not something that would be a problem, to have him to stand on a broken leg; is that right?

A.  That's not my testimony. My testimony is that I took all of the tests into consideration as I administered them, realizing that he did have a handicap.

Q.  Now, when he's standing on his broken leg with one foot in the air, he can't lean on anything or hold anything for support; is that right?

A.  That's correct.

# 9

# SENTENCING

*"Sentence first—verdict afterwards."*
LEWIS CARROLL, ALICE'S ADVENTURES IN
WONDERLAND

*"It is better to prevent crimes than punish them."*
BECCARIA

*"Man is but a free agent; were it not otherwise, priests could not
damn him."*
VOLTAIRE

*"I believe, Your Honor, it is customary to allow the defendant a few words before sentencing."*

## PROBATION REPORT
### *(Anonymous Bosch, Paris, ID)*

Given the defendant's background, it is definitely not surprising that he is currently facing his sixth commitment to the State Department of Corrections. The defendant was raised in a criminal environment, where raping, pillaging, and plundering were normal behavior.


## PROBATION REPORT
### *(Jean Farley, Ventura, CA)*

Regarding an appropriate sentence, Officer C. felt that missing a couple of Grateful Dead concerts would probably hurt the defendant more than anything.

## PROBATION REPORT
*(Steve Tapson, Placerville, CA)*

The defendant reports his future goals are to graduate from high school, and go to college. He states his primary goal was to be a police officer, but he will have to settle for being an attorney due to a felony record resulting from this present matter.

## PROBATION EVALUATION
*(Joseph Farnan, Santa Monica)*

The defendant's criminal career began over twenty years ago. He committed the present offense less than a week after being released from prison. He has now surrendered to God. God may be able to do more with this defendant than the criminal justice system has been able to do. All we mortals can do is lock him up for the maximum time allowed by the law and give God time to do His work.

## NEW MATH
*(Michael Curtis, Portland, OR)*

THE COURT　I don't think this is the kind of case that necessitates any kind of lengthy jail sentence for the defendant. It's just that—the other factors are certainly sufficient in her favor, that this is certainly not the kind of case that merits a year or eighteen months or thirty days.

I am going to impose some jail time for the case. I make it thirty days. It's my further intention to substantially reduce the time. I'm making it thirty days.

## DEFENDANTS SAY
## THE *!*!*!*!!*!*! THINGS
*(Michael Frost, Seattle)*

DEFENDANT   I am a United States citizen; I know for a fact that what I've done might piss you off. Excuse my language, but that's about to the point. But I don't particularly care. I have rights under Section 69 of the Poaching Act of 1923. By law, you can't give me more than thirteen years in prison. I shall and will be out a lot sooner to pick up where I left off. I hereby demand that you meet my requests and send me to a prison where I can hunt and fish, and also send me to an AIDS-free prison.

THE COURT   A what-free?

DEFENDANT   An AIDS-free prison. Thank you very much. *!*!*!*!!*!*.

THE COURT   Do you want to approach the lectern again, please? Do you want to repeat your last remark? I'm not sure I heard it, and I'm not sure the court reporter heard it.

DEFENDANT    Thank you very much. You *!*!*!*!!*!*.


# I AM THROUGH
*(George Taseff, Bloomington, IL)*

THE COURT    All right. The defendant is now back before this Court having not only ceased to make any effort to correct himself but having committed further criminal offenses within the Correctional Center and the defendant has come here to this Court today—

DEFENDANT    And told you you are a homosexual.

THE COURT    And affronted the dignity of this Court.

DEFENDANT    You have no dignity, you punk.

THE COURT    And has threatened to commit further acts of violence within the Department of Corrections.

DEFENDANT    Sure.

THE COURT    The Court can only conclude this defendant is a recidivist of the worst nature.

DEFENDANT    And so is your momma.

THE COURT    I'm going to sentence you to an extended term of ten years imprisonment. Do you have any questions?

DEFENDANT    Yes. Can I kick your ass?

THE COURT   No, you may not. You may take him away.

## PROBATION REPORT: TALL TALE
*(Rowan Klein, West Los Angeles)*

After numerous failures to appear at scheduled probation interviews, the defendant was finally interviewed at the Probation Office. At the time of his interview, the defendant was told that if he submitted his written statement and letters of reference, they would be attached to and made a part of this report. To date, no such statement or letters have been received.

In attempting to gain background information concerning the defendant as part of the probation interview, the defendant initially expressed reluctance in discussing his biographical information and controlled substance and alcohol use, claiming, "There is no point in going through this, I'm going to get three years [in prison]."

Regarding the offense, the defendant indicated he was seated in his parked vehicle waiting to keep an appointment. He was approached by the arresting officer who "had a beef" with him. Because of the officer's dislike of him, the defendant indicated the officer approached his vehicle, opened the car's door, and pulled him from the car.

The officer then threw the defendant to the ground, began striking him without provocation, and attempted to inject him with a syringe filled with a substance the defendant could not identify, so that he might overdose. The defendant stated he struggled to avoid being injected, but must have been struck at least once, due to the puncture wound later found on his arm and the symptoms of controlled substance use he later displayed. The defendant adamantly denied using any type of controlled substance himself that day, and he continued to deny that both the syringe and the vial belonged to him, insisting that both were the possessions of the arresting officer. Of the other items later found in his vehicle, the defendant indicated the other syringe was one which he used to treat his dog, as the dog had been seriously injured by the Police Department officers in a raid of the defendant's residence approximately one month before the recent offense. Additionally, the tablets and powder found in the car were medications for his dog, although the defendant could not recall specifically what type of medication he had been administering the dog. The sword was a part of the defendant's antique sword collection, and the keys and lockpick device were tools of his door-repair business.

The defendant indicated he has no problem with his use of controlled substances, claiming, "I don't have any habit other than crime." He further indicated, "Being a criminal is a full-time job." With respect to his idea of an appropriate disposition of the present matter, the defendant stated he should receive no punishment for the crime, as he had committed no offense. Rather, he would like to see the arresting officer submit to polygraph and psychological examinations, and he would like to file a "1983 Federal Civil Rights suit"

"Before sentencing, I'd like to thank my mom and dad, my law professors, and all the swell folks in the sixteenth congressional district who made this moment possible."

against the arresting officer. The defendant indicated his entry of a plea in the present matter was a "strategic maneuver."

## LETTER OF RECOMMENDATION
### (Earl Bute, New York City)

Dear Judge,

We understand that the defendant is awaiting your sentence for mistakes he has made. We have known him for several years, as a patient, and we feel that in spite of this terrible mistake, he has the knowledge to completely and irreversibly rehabilitate himself within the minimum sentence of eight years. He has fortunately been instructed in the Transcendental Meditation program as taught by Maharishi Mahesh Yogi, and if he will promise to practice this technology regularly twice daily during his incarceration, very quickly his brain and nervous system will become very orderly, making him incapable of disorderly thinking or action leading to crime. If he were to impress other prisoners with his progress, they might be inspired to take up the practice, and the whole prison will begin to radiate order and harmony.

## PROBATION RECOMMENDATION
*(M. Arkelian & M. Kozlow, Sacramento)*

Due to the defendant's past affiliation with the Blood Gang, it is recommended he be ordered to associate with known gang members.

## PROBATION REPORT
*(John Aquilina, Riverside, CA)*

For the past four years, the defendant and six companions earned from $500 to $4,000 a week stealing and selling cars. He intends to marry the mother of his two children in the near future and would like to eventually start his own repossession business.

## PROBATION RECOMMENDATION
*(C. David Own, Florence, AL)*

The defendant has much the same reputation in the community that one would expect Jack the Ripper or Typhoid Mary to have. In reality, those who live near him would probably prefer to have either one of the latter two. He and his brother are described as troublemakers, trash mouths, and out-and-out hoodlums.

The neighborhood lives in dread of seeing night come. It is said one never knows what will be gone when morning comes. No lawn mower, bicycle, or car battery is safe from him or his brothers.

This officer has been told that the citizens of that area chose their Christmas presents by what has the least chance of being stolen. A resident of the area stated that they are contemplating taking steps ranging anywhere from buying guns to buying dogs.

It is the feeling of this officer that he will benefit neither from probation nor incarceration. It is the feeling of this officer that he has much the same chance of successfully completing a probationary period as a naked man would have surviving in Arctic weather.

## SENTENCE OPTIONS

THE COURT    Now I suppose that with my knowledge of what goes on in the institution—and I have a lot of knowledge about that because I have been over there many times—they have their own brand of justice, you know about that, they don't have trials in the institution when they have a complaint against somebody, do they?

DEFENDANT    No, sir.

THE COURT    They take the law into their own hands, so to speak. I suppose that I could send you back over there and ask the warden just to keep hands off and let the inmates, and I am sure there are a lot of inmates over at the institution who are very unhappy over what you did here, aren't they?

| | |
|---|---|
| DEFENDANT | Yes, sir, that's right; yes. |
| THE COURT | There are lots of them who are very unhappy over what you did here. But of course that isn't my province to do that. There are other things that I have thought about. I could take the robe off, and I was a man before I was a judge, and you have heard the expression, every man has, They ought to cut something out, you know what I am talking about? |
| DEFENDANT | Yes, sir, I understand, Your Honor. |
| THE COURT | But it is not my province to resort to something like that; or to lock the doors and call the husbands of those four women down here and put you and them in here. But that isn't what I can do. There are all kinds of alternatives, but I have the unhappy position of wearing this robe, which incidentally I don't wear to bed with me, so I have to impose a penalty. |

*U.S. v. Duhart,* 496 F 2d 941 (9th Cir. 1974)

## SPEEDY SENTENCE
### *(Dave McGlaughlin, Philadelphia)*

| | |
|---|---|
| DA | This defendant along with one of the others then took money from the cash register. At that time the victim, sitting in the back of the courtroom, for |

whatever reason known only to him, attempted to get up from the floor to push the silent alarm, the burglary alarm, at which time he was shot once in the chest by one of the three and clubbed over the head with the gun, causing him to fall to the floor.

At this time his son, who was armed with a .45 automatic handgun, then jumped up from the floor and shot the first burglar once between the eyes, killing him instantly. He then turned and shot this other defendant once in the chest with the .45, and he then shot the other one once in the chest with the .45.

This defendant and the other defendant both ran out of the store and made a post-haste visit to the medical center, where the complainant was brought over there where he identified this defendant and the other one lying on a litter with IVs up their nose and in their arms.

THE COURT  Has the first burglar been sentenced?

DA  He was sentenced on the spot. He got the death penalty.

# *10*

# THE WITNESSES

*"A crook is in luck if his life depends upon his tongue and not on witnesses and proofs."*

CERVANTES

*"Come now, witness, it is most important that you give us exact details of how you spent the 12th of April last."*

*"But, Your Honor, that was nine months ago. . . ."*

*"That makes no difference . . . tell us all the same. . . ."*

HONORÉ DAUMIER, LAWYERS AND JUSTICE, NO. 17

*"Perhaps the witness would like to reconsider his answer to my question."*

## OVERHEARD*
### (Marc Blesoff, Chicago)

Q. What did you hear?

A. Just like he was—just like he was coming, you know.

Q. What sound is that, Shirley?

A. Like he ejaculated.

Q. Were there noises?

A. Yes.

Q. What kind of noises?

A. Like, ah, ahh, ahhh, ahhhhh, AHHHH, A H H H H H H H H H H, A H H H H H H H H H H H H H H H, AHHHHHHHHHHHHHHHHHH, ahhhhh, ahhh, ahh, ah.

Q. Could I ask the court reporter to read back the last three answers? I'm sorry. (Whereupon said court reporter repeated answer, falling off her chair, writhing in ecstasy.)

THE COURT        That will do, Miss Reporter. Thank you
                 very much.
COURT REPORTER   Judge, may we have a break so I could
                 have a smoke?
THE COURT        Yeah, I think we could all use one.


## BAR FLY
*(Richard Sanborn, Wichita, KS)*

Q. When you were driving on the Interstate,
   how fast were you going?
A. I never looked at the speedometer. But
   the speed limit in that part of the
   Interstate is 65 and I wasn't going 65. I
   rarely go 65.
Q. All right. I want to take us back to the
   scene of the bar for a moment again.
   (The witness starts to leave the stand.)
Q. No, you don't have to get up. I just
   want to take you back there mentally.


## WHICH DOOR?*
*(Michael Gnither, San Francisco)*

A. They was sayin', "Open the—open up
   the motherfuckin' door."
Q. What door?
A. The motherfuckin' door.

## NO SELECTIVE RECALL
*(Eleanor Schneir, Los Angeles)*

Q. Are you being selective about what you remember and what you don't remember as to the details of your previous record?

A. I don't remember.

## NOT THAT LONG
*(Mike McNew, San Diego)*

Q. And is your correct address 1845 Main?

A. Yes, it is.

Q. Do you plan on staying there for the foreseeable future?

A. Not for that long.

## FOOTLOOSE WITNESS
*(T. Jefferson Deen, III, Mobile, AL)*

Q. And how close were you?

A. We were across the bar from each other.

Q. Well, how far?

A. He was on one end and we were on the other.

Q. Way on the other end?

A. Not way on the other end, no. We were like midways of the bar.

Q.  Well, can you give me a distance in your best judgment?
A.  About like we are now.
Q.  About twelve or fifteen feet?
A.  Yes, depending on whose feet.


## MISSING IN ACTION
*(Jon Steiner, Los Angeles)*

THE COURT  Who do you have on tap for today?
PROSECUTOR  Unfortunately, one of the men who was subpoenaed for and supposed to come in for today decided to have a vasectomy today, which is an interesting way of getting out of court.


## NOBODY KNOWS MY NAME
*(Steve Cron, Santa Monica)*

Q.  So did you say that? Did you tell Deputy R. that Nobody shot about four or five times?
A.  Yes.
Q.  Did Deputy R. ask you where Nobody went after he shot?
A.  Yeah.
Q.  Smiley ran in what house and got the gun?

A. He was—he ran in Milton's house and
got the gun, so we all—after he brought
the gun back, handed it to Nobody, we
ran down the street, me and the Slob,
and the Slob started having trouble.
Nobody—Nobody shot four times.

Q. Were you standing out with Nobody?

A. Yeah. I didn't actually see who—who he
shot or nothing like that, but I know he
shot.

Q. Let me put it to you this way. When
the officer asked you, did you see the
shooting or who did the shooting, did
you answer, "Nobody"?

A. Yes.

## VICTIM INTERVIEW★
### (Mark Arnold, Woodland, CA)

A. And I seen him stand up with the gun.
I went in the living room. I set on the
couch and I knew he had a gun—and he
come out and says, "I'm not beyond
kill'n ya, you motherfucker." And I says,
"Well, shoot the gun, you son-of-a-bitch."
And he shot.

Q. You were still sitting down when he
shot?

A. I was sittin' on the couch, drinkin' a
beer—enjoying myself.

Q. Okay. How was he holding the gun when he shot? With one hand—two hands?

A. One hand.

Q. Did he aim it at you?

A. Yeah. Aimed it right—he aimed it between my eyes—he dropped it down to my stomach, and then raised it up. On the way up, it shot.

Q. Were you able to see his face when he was pointing that gun at you?

A. Yeah.

Q. Did you—did you see if he was aiming with one eye closed or had both—

A. No, he had both eyes open like a psychotic motherfucker.

Q. So it could have been an accident?

A. That motherfucker. I tell you what, I'm gonna have an accident when I get out of here. 'Cause the Police Department ain't gonna do shit. The courthouse ain't gonna do . . . Sorry about that. I gotta pee and you know what? I'm pee-shy in front of all these people. I'm laying down. I can't even—you know what? It's hard to pee when you can't see your pecker. Pardon me sir, for being so bold, but you know what? It's hard to pee when it's so damn cold.

# THE ROCK AND THE HARD PLACE*
## *(Michael Tarlton, Placerville, CA)*

Q. Did you feel anything hard in his pants that he was rubbing against you?

A. Yeah, that's how come I thought that's what it was.

Q. Then he did have an erect penis?

A. If you want to say that.

Q. I don't want to say. What do you think?

A. I'm not real sure about that.

Q. Could you tell the judge what you felt when he rubbed against you?

A. A rock, that's what it felt like. A rock, yeah.

Q. Either he had an erect penis or a rock in his pants, is that what you're saying?

# TRUE CONFESSIONS
## *(Lorin Duckman, New York City)*

Q. Do you know Mrs. O.?

A. For twenty-three years.

Q. Do you see her in court here today?

A. Yes, I do.

Q. Where is she?

A. In front of me, a little bit on the diagonal.

Q. How long have you know Mrs. O.?

A. Twenty-three years.

Q.  Are you related to her in some way by marriage?

A.  We are brother and sister-in-law.

Q.  Are you married to O.'s sister?

A.  I am married to O.'s sister by the Church, by the law, and because I am a fool.

## PERFECT ENGLISH
### (Milton Hirsch, Miami)

Q.  Do you have any problem with the English language?

A.  No. I speak very good English.

Q.  Great. Do you know Andre?

A.  That's my cousin.

Q.  You have known him all your life?

A.  Since we grewed up.

## BREAK A LEG
### (Jan David Karowsky, Sacramento)

(Whereupon, the witness's chair broke.)

MAGISTRATE  Are you all right, Officer?

WITNESS  Oh, yeah, I'm fine. The chair's not.

MAGISTRATE  I'll be darned. I've never seen that happen. The chair's broke. Can you bring one up here?

| | |
|---|---|
| COUNSEL | I've never cross-examined someone so that they fell out of the seat. |
| MAGISTRATE | Get one of the other chairs. Are you sure you're all right, Officer? |
| WITNESS | Oh, I'm fine. |
| MAGISTRATE | All right. No workers' comp claim here? |
| WITNESS | No. Tomorrow. Tomorrow when it all starts aching. |

## SAY WHAT?
*(Mark Brewer, Sarasota)*

Q. Now, do you recall the date that this accident occurred?

A. Yes, sir.

Q. What date was it?

A. It was a hot day in August.

Q. Do you drink any alcohol?

A. No, sir.

Q. Are you a teetotaler?

A. Not really. Just coffee once in a while, like in the morning.

## HISTORY'S OLDEST CRIME
*(J. Frank Mccabe, San Francisco)*

Q. Have you, any members of your family, or close friends, been arrested for any kind of crime?

A.   My brother was once arrested.
Q.   How long ago was that?
A.   Six, seven years ago.
Q.   And what was the nature of the offense?
A.   I'm not exactly sure. I think he was
     mainly arrested for being stupid.

## DEFENSE OF A DIRTY URINALYSIS*
### (Steve Rease, Monterey)

Q.   When you went in to see him on the
     18th of February, did he ask you to take
     a urine test?
A.   Yes, he did.
Q.   Did he tell you why?
A.   Not specifically. It was just at the end of
     our normal conversation he asked me to
     submit to a urinalysis. Then after giving
     him a sample, we went back to his office
     and discussed it, and at that time I had
     lied to him and told him that I was
     clean, when I knew in my mind I would
     turn up dirty. I had a situation occurred
     two days prior to the 18th that would
     prove out in this test.
Q.   So you suspected when you went on the
     18th that there could be cocaine in your
     system?
A.   Yes, sir.
Q.   How did you get the cocaine into your
     system?

A. I had picked up a woman in Monterey and we had been partying out in a bar, and she had been out earlier in the evening, and we went back to her hotel room, and we proceeded to engage in sexual intercourse and fellatio, and she had been snorting coke, and she had put coke on parts of her vagina, and I had been performing fellatio. She had coke in her mouth, which I could taste while we were French-kissing, and we left each other about eight or nine o'clock in the morning.

Q. Did you snort any cocaine that evening?

A. No, sir.

## LOCKJAW*
### (Howard Price, Beverly Hills)

Q. Anything else in terms of physical activity or lethargy that you feel is different now than it was before the accident?

A. Because of the headaches, him going to bed early or us not going out that evening.

Q. Is that why there has been an adverse effect upon your sex life?

A. No, I don't believe so.

Q. What specifically—how do I ask this

question? What specifically has been adverse about your sex life that you think has been caused by the accident?

A.   When we engage in oral sex, John has a tendency—his neck will stiffen up and his jaw will lock.

## INTIMATE EXCHANGE*
*(James Judkins, Tallahassee, FL)*

Q.   And y'all had a very intimate relationship, didn't you, Ms. A.?

A.   We had sex two times. It wasn't very intimate.

## THE ICEMAN*
*(Gene Miller, Riverside, CA)*

COUNSEL   This was the first time you had ever met the Iceman. Correct?

A.   Yes.

COUNSEL   You did have sexual intercourse with the Iceman while Jimmy was present?

A.   Uh-huh.

COUNSEL   Did the Iceman cometh?

## WHERE IS POKEY?
*(M. J. Huerta, Tampa, FL)*

A. Yeah, I used to be around with him a lot. Me and his nephew run together.

Q. Who is his nephew?

A. Pokey. I think he's doing time now.

Q. Pokey is Kenny's nephew and is doing time now? Are you saying Pokey is in the pokey?

WITNESS Yeah.


## DEDUCTIVE REASONING
*(Lloyd Stephens, San Jose)*

Q. All right. What did the individual do as far as taking property from the store without permission at that time?

A. It was right after that time when he said, "Check this out," and he pulled out his gun.

Q. All right. When you say he pulled out his gun, this would be the first guy that you were referring to?

A. Yes, sir.

Q. And when he pulled out a gun, then what happened?

A. I turned to [the other clerk] Dave and I go, "Dave, he's not going to be paying for this stuff."

## BREAK YOURSELF*
### (Earl Bute, New York City)

Q. What kind of car was he driving?

A. A green Cadillac.

Q. Was there anyone else in the car with him?

A. Yeah.

Q. Do you know that person's name?

A. No.

Q. Was he a black male, also?

A. Yes.

Q. And did you get in the car?

A. Yeah.

Q. And what happened when you got in the car?

A. We started moving. Right then he locked the door and he said, "Break yourself."

Q. Who said that?

A. Chill Will. He said, "Break yourself." That means for me to give him my money, and like if I didn't have nothing he could search me down, like pimp's arrest, you know, like, you know, check me. And I said—well, I gave him a hundred dollars.

THE COURT   You gave who a hundred dollars?

WITNESS   Chill Will.

THE COURT   Pardon?

WITNESS   Chill Will.

THE COURT   Chill Will?

WITNESS   Chill Will.

Q. That's the person you have identified here in court?

A. Yeah.

THE COURT Why did you give him the hundred dollars?

WITNESS Because I was in his car, right? I mean, I got in the car, and when you are in a pimp's car, like, see, I didn't have no money, but I did, but I am hiding it. If I get in his car, he can say, "Break yourself." And if I don't give him my money, he can search me, go up inside me with his fingers, whatever.

THE COURT What made you believe he was a pimp?

WITNESS I didn't really at first. Not at first I didn't.

Q. What later made you believe he was a pimp?

A. Because he locked all the doors and said, "Break yourself."

## MINOR WITNESS
### (Bruce Schweiger, Los Angeles)

Q. Who was the other male who was with you?

A. It is a relative of ours who is there who lives with my family.

Q. Do you know what his name is?

A. Just his name, "Minor."

Q. His name is "Minor"?

A. "Minor," yeah.

Q. Do you know what his last name is?

A. No, I don't know.

Q. Do you know how old Minor is?

A. He is the one that I tell you that I think he is a minor but I am not sure.

Q. So Minor is a minor, okay?

A. Minor is a man.

## NAMING NAMES*
### (Ira Loewy, Miami)

Q. Yes. Would you also agree with me, Miss, that you never used the name "Charles" on any of those tapes?

A. Yes.

Q. And your explanation for that is that you had a nickname for Charles. You called him "Biggums"; is that correct?

A. Yes.

Q. Did your friend on the tape call Charles "Biggums," too?

A. Sometimes.

Q. Sometimes he did and sometimes he didn't?

A. Yes.

Q. What did he call him when he wasn't calling him "Biggums"?

A. "Motherfucker."

## TOPIC OF INTEREST★
*(Kenneth Quigley, San Francisco)*

DA    What were you talking about before you had sex, if anything?

Counsel    Objection, vague. With whom? When?

The Court    I am going to sustain the objection. I think that's already been asked and answered. She talked about the conversation already. You asked her about the sex at this point. Let's get back to the sex.

Counsel    Did you ever accuse him of falsely imprisoning you at the Henry Hotel?

A.    What's falsely imprisoning you?

Q.    Holding you against your will.

A.    He's the father of my baby. He ain't never falsely did nothing to me.


## TAKING OATH SERIOUSLY
*(Robert Fracchia, Fairfield, CT)*

Q.    Okay. Do you understand what the oath means, taking the oath means?

A.    No.

Q.    You don't?

A.    No, I don't.

Q.    Did you take an oath today in court?

A.    What is that? I don't understand what's oath like.

Q.   Well, the oath is like when you raise
     your hand and swear to tell the truth.
A.   Yeah.
Q.   Okay. Do you remember doing that
     today?
A.   Yeah.
Q.   Okay. You understand what that means?
A.   Yes.
Q.   What does that mean?
A.   That means to say the truth, the whole
     truth.
Q.   And what happens if you don't tell the
     truth?
A.   I should be executed.


## BIG MEAL
*(Sheldon Breier, West Los Angeles)*

COURT CLERK   Please state your name and spell your last
              name.
THE COURT     She has already been sworn.
COURT CLERK   She is a different one. I am sorry, Your
              Honor. She looks different.
WITNESS       I ate.

## POST-LUNCH CROSS
### (Bob Goldman, Martinez, CA)

Q. Is there anything that you had at lunch that would in any way interfere with your ability to give answers truthfully and correctly this afternoon?

A. Hamburger?

Q. I'm just asking if there's anything else.

A. No.

Q. I assume you did not imbibe any alcoholic beverages?

A. No, I didn't.

Q. Did your attorney?

A. No, he didn't.

Q. Maybe he should have.


## NUMB FROM THE NECK UP
### (Edward Witt Chandler, Memphis)

COUNSEL    And then when you got to the grand jury, when they cross-examined you, after you got your immunity, you said that you were a drunkard at that time; that you were brain dead; and you didn't really remember what happened. Isn't that the truth?

WITNESS    Would you rephrase that, please?

COUNSEL    Your own words. You described yourself as being a drunkard and being brain dead.

WITNESS    You ever been drunk for a year?
COUNSEL    Yes, sir.
WITNESS    Were you not brain dead at the time?
COUNSEL    No, sir—you're asking me?
WITNESS    Yes.
COUNSEL    No, sir, I've never been brain dead.
WITNESS    Believe me, your brain is numb after being drunk for a year.

## CARNAL KNOWLEDGE
*(Hon. Bruce S. Jenkins, Salt Lake City)*

Mr. D., an old practitioner, tells of talking to a rather coarse client. She was a witness in a Mann Act case. He tried to clean up her language. He gave her an acceptable word to replace a common word of Anglo-Saxon fame. The prosecutor on cross was unbelieving of her newfound respectable vocabulary.

"Do you know what intercourse is?" he asked. "I never knew what intercourse was until I met Mr. D.," she replied.

## ANOTHER POSITIVE IDENTIFICATION

At an assault hearing in Detroit's 36th District Court on Wednesday, [a] shooting victim was asked to pick out his alleged assailant . . . who was sitting in the last row of spectators.

He strolled the courtroom, peering into faces, until he paused near the back row. "He said, 'That's him,' and just reached over two rows and wopped my client right in the face," said defense lawyer Wright Blake.

Assistant Prosecutor Michael Callahan said, "I asked that the record reflect that the complainant has identified the defendant."

*Detroit Free Press, 7/29/90*


## I'LL NEVER FORGET
## THAT FACE (EXCEPT TODAY)
### (Andrew D. Levy, Baltimore)

| | |
|---|---|
| DA | I want you to look around the courtroom and see if you see Sweetsy in the courtroom today. |
| WITNESS | No. |
| DA | Okay. Do you know someone by the name of Willie Reid? |
| WITNESS | No. |
| DA | You don't see him here today, either? |
| WITNESS | No. |
| DA | Are you certain about that? Stand up and walk around and see if you see anybody. |
| THE COURT | Look at the people at the trial table there, right where the lawyers are; look at them. |
| WITNESS | Oh! |
| DA | All right. Now you said, "Oh!" Did you see someone you recognized? |

WITNESS  Yes.
DA     And who did you see?
WITNESS  Sweetsy.
DA     Let the record reflect he is indicating the defendant, Willie Reid.

From *Reid v. State*, 501 A.2d 436, 442 n.3 (1985)

## ANIMAL, BEAR, AND STEVE*
### (Mark Arnold, Woodland, CA)

Q. Who else was there besides Steve and Animal? Or can you describe Animal for me? What's he look like?
A. Shit. He looks like an animal.
Q. Looks like an animal?
A. This hairy dude.
Q. He's hairy?
A. Yeah.
Q. A beard?
A. Yeah, he's got a lot of beard.
Q. Any idea about how old he is, how tall, his weight?
A. I don't know, I will tell you, I just barely met him. I met Steve and gave him a ride and I met them guys.
Q. Who else was there?
A. Just Animal and Bear and Steve.
Q. Bear? That's different than Animal?
A. Yeah?
Q. What did Bear look like?

A. Like a bear. Just a hairy dude, you know, just hairy.

COUNSEL They are all hairy.


# DON'T LEAVE HOME WITHOUT IT*
## (Mark Kaiserman, Santa Monica)

Q. Now, at some point did she tell you to tell Milano to bring his butt here?

A. Yes.

Q. And did you do that?

A. Yes.

Q. When?

A. I don't know. Sometime we living in Sherman Oaks and she wanted him to come spend time with her. And she said, "If Milano call, tell him to bring his butt here." And I told him like that.

Q. Did he do it?

A. Well, he can't leave home without it.
(Later)

Q. At the time that you identified the picture of Mr. M., do you recall what you told the detectives regarding that picture at that time?

A. Yeah, the same thing I just told you.

Q. That he was good-looking?

DA I'm not good-looking?

A. When you put a toupee on.

COUNSEL You asked for it.

THE COURT They're sworn to tell the truth in here.

## AND A GOOD BUNCH AT THAT
### (David Fuller, Santa Rosa)

Q. How did you know that it was February 12 that you were working on your car at Chris's house?

A. Because I went over there and I talked to a bunch of my alibis that I'm hanging around with.

Q. Bunch of who?

A. Alibis, the bunch of people I always hang around with.

## SHOOTING BLANKS
### (Lance J. Rogers, Washington, DC)

Q. Do you know the accused in this case?

A. Yes, I do.

Q. If she's present, would you point to her and state her name?

A. (Pointing at the accused) It's, uh, uh, Airman uh—I've got so many. Uh, what's her name?

Q. Are you drawing another blank today?

From *U.S. v. Kirk,* 31 *Military Justice Reporter,* 86 (CMA 1990)

## TOTAL RECALL
### (Jeanne Keevan-Lynch, San Francisco)

DA  Did your son tell you before he came in here what day it was?

WITNESS  No, he didn't tell me, but I myself know.

DA  Did your granddaughter talk to you about it?

WITNESS  No, sometimes when I'm sober and working around the house, I remember these things.


## ON BEING A PROFESSIONAL*
### (Michael Chaney, West Hollywood)

DA  How would your pimp tell you it was time to get to work?

A.  It would depend on his attitude that day, how he was talking to whomever he was talking to in particular. Like one morning in particular he said something like, "It's time to get up and start whoeing."

DA  Whoeing? And what does whoeing mean?

A.  It means going to work as a prostitute. Some people refer to it as "whoring," but women in our profession don't refer to it as "whoring." We refer to it as "whoeing." There's a big difference.

DA  And what is the difference between whoeing and whoring?

A.  Well, we consider ourselves professionals, and we're doing it for money. Any normal woman can go out and be a whore and not receive any money for it.

DA  So the distinction is that whoeing is for money?

A.  And whoring isn't.

DA  Did you ask your pimp how far police could go in making arrests?

A.  Yes, I did.

DA  What was said?

A.  I asked how can a police officer get naked and then arrest a working girl?

DA  What did he say?

A.  He said that they were cold-blooded and that they loved their jobs because they probably just wanted to see some pussy.

DA  What did he tell the other girl that she had to do?

A.  He told her it was time to rise and shine and get whoeing.

DA  Get whoeing. Okay.

THE COURT  How is that spelled?

DA  Whoeing?

THE COURT  H-O-W-I-N-G? I think we need that clarified for the record.

WITNESS  W-H-O-E-I-N-G.

THE COURT  W-H-O-E-I-N-G. Thank you.

## WORKING GIRL MEETS PIMP*
### (Ken Quigley, San Francisco)

Q. What, if anything, did the defendant say when he approached you on the night of April 14?

A. He just called me about a hundred bitches.

Q. Can you remember his exact words?

A. Not really, no.

Q. And what did you say to him?

A. I must say, I did cuss him out pretty good.

Q. Could you give us your exact words?

A. My exact words?

Q. Yes.

A. Why you thirteen-dollar no-account, you couldn't get close enough to my pussy to smell it, much less get your dick in it.


## THE BIG SLEEP WALKER
### (Milton Hirsch, Miami)

Q. Bringing your attention to an incident that occurred that night near the intersection of West 8th and Okeechobee, can you tell us what you saw that night regarding the death of a man at that location?

WITNESS Okay. I witnessed when the dead man was crossing the street.

## SHIT GEORGE IS NOT MY NAME*
### (David Carleton, Los Angeles)

THE COURT     Billy, is that your true name, or is it
              George?
DEFENDANT     You should know, you the judge, ain't
              you?
THE COURT     Yeah, but I wasn't there when your mom
              and dad gave you the name. That's why
              I'm asking you the question.
DEFENDANT     My correct name is Billy. I don't know
              where they get that shit George.
THE COURT     We'll let the record reflect that Billy says
              Shit George is not his true name.


## ANOTHER DAY AT THE OFFICE
### (Steve Blake, San Diego)

Q.   What do you do as a clerk?
A.   I work as a cashier and, you know,
     sometimes I make the orders and, you
     know, deliveries sometimes. Everything in
     the store.
Q.   Now, directing your attention again to
     June 16, did something unusual happen
     inside the liquor store on that day?
A.   No. Everything was regular.
Q.   Everything was normal?
A.   Normal. Yeah.

Q. Well, was there a body found inside the liquor store on that day?

A. Yeah, that's right.

## TIME IS SHORT
*(Delgado Smith, Texarkana, TX)*

THE COURT  I understand we have a short witness next?

COUNSEL  Yes. (Calls witness) Sir, would you face the jury and tell the jury how tall are you?

A. Five nine.

Q. Thank you, sir. Those are all the questions I have.

## HOSTILE WITNESS*
*(Jay F. Huntington, New Haven, CT)*

Q. Would it be fair to say that there is, or was, a great deal of bad blood between Roger and Jose and your children?

A. I have no idea. Only argument that there was, Jose was mad because Roger asked Jose's mother to go to bed with him.

Q. Say what?

A. The only reason was because he asked Jose's mother to go to bed with him.

Q. Who asked whose mother to go to bed?

A. Roger asked.

Q. Roger asked Jose's mother to go to bed?

A. Yes.

Q. Okay. Anything else you want to throw in here at this point?

A. No. There's nothing else.

Q. Was Roger involved in the Lindbergh kidnapping or the invasion of Kuwait?

DA Your Honor, I object. I'd ask that be stricken.

WITNESS Why don't you ask him? He's your client.

# 11

# POTPOURRI

"If we desire respect for the law, we must first make the law respectable."

LOUIS BRANDEIS

"But do not give it to a lawyer's clerk to write, for they use a legal hand that Satan himself will not understand."

CERVANTES

"A drunk man is as much entitled to a safe street as a sober one, and much more in need of it."

ROBINSON V. PIOCHE, 5 CAL. 461, 462 (1855)

*"We're hopelessly deadlocked—six of us grew up on 'Perry Mason' and six of us grew up on 'L.A. Law.'"*

# POPE GETS TWENTY-THREE YEARS

"What's in a name?" inquired Shakespeare's most celebrated heroine; and appellant Napoleon Elijah Pope may well be asking the same question, with four felony convictions already to his credit; appellant, bearer of names rich in connotations of temporal and spiritual power and glory, was found guilty on a charge of theft by taking and sentenced to twenty-three years imprisonment.

*State v. Pope,* Ga Ct. of Appeals

# MAYOR MUTT
*(Richard Krech, Oakland, CA)*

A. Well, I mean they are collies. They are trained. I mean the dogs are trained. I don't watch them every minute.

Q. Do you let them roam free out where you live?

A.  Yes, I do now. We live in Sunol. I don't know if you know the area. Our mayor is a dog. Our newly elected official is a dog.

Q.  Is he on a leash?

A.  He does not wear a leash, no.


## WHAT WILL HAPPEN?
### (David Hazelkorn, Santa Ana)

*Daily Variety*'s Army Archerd reports that the ABC-TV remake of Robert Aldrich's 1962 Bette Davis-Joan Crawford film, *Whatever Happened to Baby Jane?* (which just finished shooting with Vanessa and Lynn Redgrave as the feuding sisters) may not be able to bear the same title as the original.

The Aldrich family owns the rights to the *Whatever Happened to . . . ?* part, but Warner Bros. owns the *Baby Jane* part. So far, the sides representing the two crucial parts of the title have been unable to reach an agreement.


## A CLASSIC PRONOUNCEMENT
### (Roger Shuy, Washington, DC)

Some weeks ago, one of our High Courts delivered a judgment in Sanskrit. Perhaps these things are taken in its stride by a land in which legal work was conducted in Persian during the Mogul period, and then

in English when the British arrived, and where sur-
prises are sprung by language enthusiasts every so often.
Curiosity impelled me, however, to go deeper into the
matter, and what turned up might be of some interest
to lawyers and future litigants.

It appears that there was a quarrel about rent or
something between an Iranian student and his landlord, a Tamilian settled in Allahabad. The former filed
a writ petition in Persian. At the preliminary hearing,
the judge suggested that it would be convenient for all
concerned if the documents were submitted in either
English or Hindi. The foreign student submitted that
since he could express himself best in Persian, he would
feel more confident about the course of justice if his
plea in that language was accepted.

The Iranian said he would have only one witness, a
Sri Lankan friend, also a temporary resident in India.
At the next hearing, that witness submitted an affidavit
in Sinhala to affirm what he knew about the facts of the
complainant's grievances. It was apprehended that this
might spark off a political controversy but mercifully
such fears were set at rest when the landlord cited a
Christian priest as his sole witness. The judge scratched
his head discreetly under the wig when this man of God
contended that since all his religious training had been
in Latin, his affidavit would also have to be in that
language. He also cited the fact that the English used
in the Indian Penal Code, as also in all books on juris-
prudence, was half Latin in any case.

When the case came up next, the judge asked for
copies of Sinhala-English, Latin-Hindi, Tamil-Persian
and Sinhala-Tamil dictionaries to be placed before the

court within a fortnight. Both counsels asked for three months time, which was granted. At the end of that period, and not without great difficulty, the four tomes were produced, and were marked Exhibits 1, 2, 3, and 4, respectively. It was expected that the proceedings would hereafter proceed smoothly, but a new complication was introduced when the Iranian student made another plea to the court, this time begging permission to engage another lawyer (to assist the senior counsel), and to allow him to address the court in Arabic which, he said, formed a regular course of studies in most Indian universities, and was therefore a recognized language.

Not to be out-maneuvered, the Tamil landlord made a similar request for hiring a junior counsel to argue his side of the case, adding that the man would do so in Sindhi. He pointed out that this too was an approved language, as was evident from the fact that Akashvani broadcast daily programs in that language. Both the requests were granted. If sources close to the judge are to be believed, by then he had begun to enjoy it all.

No newspaper reported this, but on the day the judgement was to be delivered, the court was full of orientalists from all over the country, and many from abroad too. There was a hush when the judge entered, took his seat, looked around and said cryptically that he wished someone from Varanasi had also been present. He then proceeded to read out the 37-page judgement in Sanskrit.

H. R. Luthra, *Indian Express*, 12/16/85, Bangalore, India

# NAVY JETS ATTACK
# PUBLIC DEFENDER
*(Gerald Farber, Victorville, CA)*

Two Navy fighter jets were unable to keep David Menezes San Bernardino deputy public defender away from his appointed rounds at the Trona Justice Court on Wednesday. It seems that Mr. Menezes was en-route to the Justice Court on the Trona Randsburg Road when two screaming jets pounced upon his County vehicle at tree top level. The first jet swooped in unseen. Mr. Menezes felt that he was about to be hit by a semi, but could not see another vehicle on the road. Then the second jet swooped in and ignited its afterburners, which sent a supersonic concussion into his vehicle. The effect of the two jets caused the driver to lose control of his vehicle, cross both lanes of traffic and leave the road. The vehicle sustained two ruptured tires and dented rims. Otherwise, the sworn deputy was unscathed.

*Trona Argonaut*, 7/6/90

# NOT TO BE TONGUE-TIED

The following anecdote illustrates the need of cau-tion: O'Regan's Memoirs of John Philpott Curran, 29: "An Irish witness, Mr. Curran said, was called on the table to give evidence, and having a preference for his own language (first, as that in which he could best ex-press himself, next, as being a poor Celt he loved it for its antiquity, but above all other reasons, that he could better escape cross-examination by it), and wishing to appear mean and poor and therefore a mere 'Irish,' he was observed on coming into court to take the buckles [tongues] cunningly out of his shoes. The reason of this was asked by counsel, and one of the country people, his opponent in the suit, cried out, 'The reason, my lord, is that the fellow does not like to appear to be *master of two tongues!*' "

Recounted in *3 Wigmore on Evidence*, 3rd edn., section 81, p. 225, n. 1

## THE OBEDIENT WITNESS
### *(Larry Ainbinder, San Diego)*

Q.    I'm going to ask you a series of questions and this gentleman in front of you is writing it all down. He's only able to write down audible responses, so you can't shake your head up and down or shake it across to designate no or yes. All right?

A.    (Nods head affirmatively).

## DISABILITY FROM NOSE BLOWING WHILE AT WORK IS COMPENSABLE

Fountain Valley Police Officer Michael Freil endured a bizarre sequence of mishaps. On duty and suf-

"So it is your contention that when you opened the cupboard to remove the bone, it was already missing."

fering from a head cold, he blew his nose in the restroom of the city garage. He then became dizzy and
nauseated. Freil called for help, and his supervisor took
him to the hospital. There the officer was given an
anti-nausea medication. The medical examiner determined the drug caused a stroke which permanently dis-
abled Freil from police work.

Is the officer entitled to a service-connected dis-
ability retirement? YES.

*Freil v. Worker's Compensation Appeals Board,* 227 Cal. App. 3d 496, 498 (1991)

## SHAKEOUT
### (Janice Feinstein, Los Angeles)

Unusual interest has been manifested in the case
by the Chinese residents of this city, on account of
the record of the defendant. The latter was convicted
before Judge Lawlor of San Francisco for the crime
of murder and sentenced to ninety-nine years in prison.
The Supreme Court granted a new trial owing to errors
in the instruction of the Court to the jury. Before the
defendant could be tried a second time the earthquake
and big fire occurred, and the records in the case were
destroyed, necessitating a release of the defendant.

From *People v. Wong Luong,* 159 Cal. 520 (1911)

## A FAMILIAR ADDRESS
*(R. William Schooley, Ann Arbor, MI)*

THE COURT   Is Ms. K. present?

COUNSEL   Good morning, Your Honor. This is the day scheduled for her sentencing in this prostitution matter. I am unable to explain her absence from the Court.

THE COURT   All right, the defendant not appearing, her bond will be forfeited and a warrant issued.

COUNSEL   Your Honor, the last phone number I had for her, I believe, was the Your Motel. Does the Court have a phone number different than 555-9081?

THE COURT   Well, I see she has an address in Belleville. The Your Motel may be a business address.

COUNSEL   I would hope not.


## HOW MANY MACARONI?
*(Tom Adler, San Diego)*

Q.   I'd like now to turn to the day of the incident, December 20. Can you briefly describe what you did that day, if you remember?

A.   What do you mean? All day?

Q.   Yeah.

A.   I did what I always do.

Q. Do you remember about what time you got up?

A. No.

Q. Did you have lunch that day?

A. Yeah.

Q. Do you remember what you had?

A. No.

Q. Okay. How about dinner? Did you have dinner?

A. Yes.

Q. What did you have for dinner?

A. I think it was macaroni and cheese and chicken.

Q. And can you describe the portions that you had?

A. You want to know if I'm a pig? Yeah. I had a lot. I don't know how to describe a portion.

Q. Okay. Did you cook your dinner yourself?

COUNSEL A. Oh, my God, Counsel. What does that have to do with anything? Come on. Please tell me.

COUNSEL B. Sure. If you've got one of those little packages of macaroni and cheese—he knows how much he put in there. I'm just trying to get an idea of portions. I don't know.

COUNSEL A. Whether he cooked the macaroni and cheese?

COUNSEL B. If he would know what kind of portions there were. The questions were: What size portions?

COUNSEL A.   I thought he said he ate a lot.

COUNSEL B.   And he said he ate like a pig, and I'm trying to get an idea what he means by that.

COUNSEL A.   Did you cook dinner, Bob?

WITNESS   No.

COUNSEL B.   When you said you ate like a pig, is there any other way you can describe that?

A.   I ate a lot.

Q.   Did you have more than one piece of chicken?

A.   I don't remember. I'm sure I did.

Q.   Did your wife cook dinner for you that night?

A.   I think.

Q.   If your wife didn't do it, who would have cooked your dinner?

A.   My mother. One or the other cooks dinner every night.

Q.   Brother or wife?

A.   Mother.

Q.   Back to the question of how much you ate. When you ate dinner, was it all on a plate, or was it like in a TV dinner?

COUNSEL A.   Counsel, are you actually serious about that question? I mean, are you really serious about it? Are you suggesting because he had one beer, he was under the influence of alcohol because of the amount of food that he ate on the plate because of a TV dinner?

COUNSEL B. That certainly could have relevance as to how much he ate, yes.

COUNSEL A. Well, I'll let him answer it, but, Counsel, I'll tell you, this is about as far as I'm going to go with TV dinners. He was not charged. He had no blood alcohol in him. What kind of plate he used when he ate? I'm not going to allow that kind of questioning to go on. I'll stop the deposition if you do it. He said he ate like a pig. I think anyone in their right mind knows he ate a lot. How else can you remember in December of 1989 how much macaroni he ate other than he ate like a pig? Do you want to count the number of macaroni? I mean, this is ridiculous.

COUNSEL B. (TO THE WITNESS) Well, let me ask you some further questions. I see that you're smiling, and I don't blame you, but these questions I do have to ask. Do you know whether or not the macaroni was in one of those little Kraft containers?

A. I'm sure it wasn't.

Q. Do you think that the best person to know how much you ate was your mother?

A. No.

Q. It would be whoever cooked it for you?

A. No. It would be me. I ate it.

Q. You said that you probably had more than one piece of chicken; is that true?

A. Yeah.

Q. Would you have had more than two?

A. I'm not sure.

Q. Could you have had as many as three pieces of chicken that night?

Counsel A. I'm going to object, it's speculative.

Q. When you ate dinner, you ate it on a plate.

Counsel A. As opposed to the floor, Counsel?

Counsel B. We're back to TV dinners. I'm trying to get an idea as to the plate, was it a little compartment that had food for various areas? I mean, there's all kinds of areas that he could have—

Counsel A. As to whether he ate it on a plate.

Counsel B. As opposed to a TV dinner carton.

Witness It wasn't a TV dinner.

Counsel B. It was on a plate?

A. Uh-huh.

Q. Would it be accurate to say your plate was full?

A. I guess.

Counsel A. Did your cup runneth over? Are we just about done, Counsel, with the macaroni issue?

Counsel B. Yes, yes.